THE
BUTTERFLIES OF CEYLON

THE BUTTERFLIES OF CEYLON

W. ORMISTON

GYAN

Published by

Gyan Publishing House
5, Ansari Road
Daryaganj, New Delhi-110002
Phone: 011-47034999, 9811692060
E-mail: books@gyanbooks.com

Distribution Network
gyanbooks.com
India, USA, Canada, UK, Australia, France

ISBN : 978-81-212-4504-3 (HB)
First Published, Colombo 1924

2nd Impression 2020

Printed at: Gyan Press, Delhi.

THE BUTTERFLIES OF CEYLON

By

W. ORMISTON, F.E.S.

Printed & Published by

H. W. CAVE & Co., COLOMBO

1924

PREFACE

My notes on the butterflies of Ceylon were published in " Spolia Zeylanica " in 1918-19, and Dr. Pearson, the Director of the Colombo Museum, suggested that they should be revised and issued as a Museum publication. Since then I have spent two years in England, and have been able to examine the collections in the British Museum (Natural History), and to consult many books which were not available in Ceylon, with the result that the greater portion of the notes have been entirely rewritten. Unfortunately when the manuscript was ready for the printers, the Ceylon Government found that they were unable, for financial reasons, to carry out their scheme, and I am compelled to publish it without their assistance.

The great work on Ceylon Butterflies is Moore's "Lepidoptera of Ceylon," a copy of which is kept at most of the Kachcheries for the benefit of collectors. It was published more than 40 years ago, and a great deal has been learnt since then, and this book is only intended as a supplement, to bring it, as far as possible, up-to-date. Moore gives coloured plates of almost every butterfly then known, I therefore only illustrate those discovered since his work appeared.

As he mainly uses sub-generic names I give these in brackets, *e.g.: Danaida* (*Parantica*) *aglea;* most of these are unnecessary and are no longer used.

The other leading authorities, in order of date, are:—

1st. " The Butterflies of India, Burma and Ceylon," by Col. Marshall and De Niceville.

2nd. " Fauna of India: Butterflies," by Col. Bingham.

3rd. " A list of Indian Butterflies," by Lt.-Col. Evans.

I mention the names given by all these, giving the authority after each, *viz.:* M. = Moore's "Lepidoptera of Ceylon." De N = De Nicéville; B = Bingham, and E = Evans.

Moore's "Lepidoptera Indica" is well illustrated and is the leading authority on species not dealt with yet in the "Fauna of India: Butterflies." Its cost (£86) is, however, prohibitive, and I do not know of a copy in Ceylon. Another authority is Seitz "Macrolepidoptera of the World," which is now appearing in parts. The illustrations are good, but the letterpress is very scanty. It can be consulted at the Colombo Museum.

The greatest difficulty in naming our forms lies in deciding whether they are species, sub-species or races, varieties, or aberrations. In this I have tried to follow an article by Dr. T. A. Chapman, M.D., F.E.S. (Entomologist's Record, Vol. XXX., p. 168). He writes:—"One has to use words that are not definitely accepted by every one in the same sense. For present purposes I use 'race' or 'sub-species' for the inhabitants of two different areas, if they can be distinguished.......... The race inhabiting the locality from which the type of the species comes, retains the type name, which is also that of any race indistinguishable from it.

"A 'variety' is a form occurring with the type race, or anywhere else, in fair numbers suggesting that it is usual for the species to vary in this way. An 'aberration' differs from a variety in being comparatively rare and unusual, and suggestive of probably having a pathological cause. The line of demarcation between 'variety' and 'aberration' may not always be easy to draw........... ....I think a sub-species is a sub-species whether its geographical separation be complete or not, even if there be no very stringent separation at all. Of course, geographical separation is almost conclusive proof that the separated race is a sub-species, and if this be so, then it seems unnecessary to find any varietal differences, though as a matter of fact, such differences practically always exist where races are so separated. The real proof that geographical races are sub-species, or that any two different races of a species are sub-species, is not to be found in their segregation, or in the amount of their differences, but in the circumstance, that these differences have a permanence under any disturbance as of habitat, etc., that makes some approach to the permanence under such disturbance of a species. That this can rarely be ascertained makes it necessary that we should observe a doubtful attitude in most cases, admitting that we are unable to decide in either way, unless so strong a fact as geographical separation obtains.''

For example:—

1. Moduza Calidasa. This is peculiar to Ceylon, but is closely allied to *M. procris* of India. It is found at all elevations, and in both the wet and dry zones, but I believe that no varieties approaching *M. procris* are known. The differences are apparently permanent, and it is well separated geographically: I therefore give it specific rank.

2. Papilio aristolochiae ceylonica. Also confined to Ceylon and found all over the Island. Variations approaching *P. aristolochiae* are numerous, and specimens are occasionally found indistinguishable from that species. It is well separated geographically, but the differences are not permanent: I therefore treat it as a race, or sub-species.

3. Surendra quercetorum var. discalis. The name *discalis* has been given to the Ceylon form. De Nicéville writes: "It is simply a small form of *S. quercetorum;* it has absolutely, as far as I can see, no other character by which it can be distinguished.''........ "Even size is not sufficient to distinguish *S. quercetorum*, as I possess some specimens of that species from Sikkim, which are quite as small as any *Surendra* from S. India, Ceylon, or the Andamans.''

It varies appreciably in size in Ceylon. This form is neither permanent nor geographically separated, and I therefore treat it as a variety.

It is of course quite impossible to draw up any rule to fix at what stage in its development a variety becomes a race, or a race becomes a species. This must be left to the opinion of each individual writer. At present the tendency is to treat every form as a local race, if possible.

This shows the importance of collecting all varieties, especially those which tend to connect our forms with Indian ones, and I would especially impress upon beginners the importance of labelling every specimen accurately with locality and date of capture.

I have often been asked what good the study of butterflies can do from an economic point of view. For answer I give what I fear is a very incomplete list of our butterflies, the larvæ of which are known to feed on cultivated plants. It may be true that, with the exception of *L. elpis*, which attacks cardamoms, none are at present known to be serious pests in Ceylon. Many feed on rice but their numbers seem to be kept in check by natural enemies; should, however, any slight change in the balance of Nature arise they might seriously affect the food supply of the Island. Even now, though the damage done in each field may be small, in the aggregate the loss must be very large. About one-tenth of our forms feed on grasses or paddy or both. They can be divided into four groups:—1st. Those which eat paddy for preference but can flourish on grasses when the rice crop is over. 2nd. Those which eat grasses for preference, but will attack paddy when the grass is dried up by a drought. 3rd. Those which eat grasses or paddy indiscriminately, and 4th. Those which feed on grass only. From my limited observations I would put *A. maro* in the first group, *P. colaca* in the second, and *M. leda* in the third. I know no representative of the 4th class for certain. If any one wishes to take up the study of butterflies from the economic point of view I could recommend no better subject for him to start on.

I have been asked to include instructions for preserving butterflies in this volume. I would recommend beginners to purchase one of the numerous handbooks on the subject, which treat it fuller and more ably than I could do. Dr. Knagg's "Lepidopterist's Guide" is one of the best.

Mr. T. Bainbrigge-Fletcher, the Indian Imperial Entomologist, read a paper on collecting in India at the Entomological Congress held at Pusa in February, 1919, and this has been issued as a Departmental Bulletin of the Indian Agricultural Research Institute; it can be bought for a few cents. Lt.-Col. W. H. Evans has also just published an excellent paper on the same subject in the Journal of the Bombay Natural History Society, which I hope will be reprinted and put on sale.

The great enemies of collectors in Ceylon are mould and mites, and a liberal use of Naphthalene is the best protection. Should mould appear, a small wad of cotton wool damped with Formalin may be pinned in the box for 24 to 48 hours; this will kill the mould which can then be removed with a fine camel's hair brush.

Very little has so far been done in breeding our forms, and even the larva of *Appias paulina*, almost our commonest butterfly, is still unknown. The most satisfactory method of breeding is to induce a female to lay eggs in captivity. This can be done by growing the food plant in a flowerpot in a cage of mosquito netting. Catch the female with as little injury as possible, and feed her regularly with jaggery, toddy, or rotten fruit. The resulting larvæ can then be divided and reared under different conditions of light and shade, moisture of food, etc., in the hope of breeding wet and dry season, or other forms. The parent must be preserved for comparison, even though she is almost invariably badly battered. Unfortunately many butterflies refuse to lay eggs in captivity.

A large collection when set up unfortunately requires a lot of boxes and takes up a lot of room, so many collectors only keep a very limited number of each species. From a scientific point of view it would be far better to collect one or two genera only and work them thoroughly.

Butterflies can be studied anywhere in the Island, though only a few species could be expected in a district like Hatton where there is little jungle or waste land. Bandarawella is also a poor district, but is a good centre for the study of the genus *Aphnæus* and paddy pests. In a circle with Haldummulla Post Office as its centre, and a radius of 5 miles, I have personally taken, in 30 years collecting, over 200 forms out of the 240 mentioned in these notes and of these I have taken over 60 in every month of the year. The best places I know for a collector to go to in order to make a fairly complete collection in a short time are:—1st. Wellawaya Resthouse, in the province of Uva. About 160 species may be taken there including the rarities *E. nais*, *L. lepita lepitoides*, *C. lithargyria*, *N. dana* and *noreia*, *C. nilgirica*, *V. perse*, *C. siamica*, and *B. sena*. The best months are March, April, July, November, and December. 2nd. Kandy. This is the headquarters of the native collectors who bring large numbers of the commoner butterflies to the Queen's Hotel for sale. If paid sufficient they may bring *H. onyx cingalensis*, *G. thyrsis*, *P. lebadea*, *B. sena*, *etc.* They usually ask for money in advance and the majority are not to be trusted. July and August are good months. 3rd. Nuwara Eliya for Hill forms. 4th. Ratnapura, Kottawa, Deniyaya, etc., for wet zone forms. The best place is in the Hills north of the Ratnapura-Balangoda road. The rarities to be taken there include *L. dynsate*, *M. rama*, *D. lepida*, *A. abseus mackwoodi*, *R. lankana*, *A. indra narendra*, *H. nadina remba*, *P. antiphates alcibiades*, *H. decorata*, *P. penicillata*, *T. thwaitesi*, *etc.* The majority of these with the addition of *A. ormistoni* and *H. onyx cingalensis*, may be taken in the jungles between Kottawa and Deniyaya. The latter place has been very little worked so far. 5th. Murunkan Resthouse, near Mannar, for dry zone forms. *C. fausta tripuncta*, *C. eucharis*, and *danae*, *B. ilithyia*, *A. ubaldus*, *V. isocrates*, *S. nubilus*, *S. lunulifera fairliei*, *etc.*, are common there. The best months are November, December, and July. *T. jehana ceylanica* and *R. melampus* and other good dry zone forms may be taken in the same months at Kankesanturai, near Jaffna. The North of the Island has been very little worked, and new species should be found there. Other good collecting centres are Trincomalie, Dambool, Tissamaharama, Madampe, Elephant Pass and Tangalle.

The best baits I know are: 1st. Small pieces of sponge soaked in toddy, in which a little jaggery has been dissolved. Pin these to trees, or lay them on rocks in likely places. A screw top jam bottle is the best thing to carry them in. Squirrels are very fond of toddy, and will eat the sponges if left unwatched. 2nd. Treacle, or jaggery boiled in beer, with a good dash of rum added just before use. This is best for *Kallima* and *Charaxes*. 3rd. Overripe fruit, especially jak. This is best for *Discophora*. 4th. A dead specimen, pinned on a twig, will often attract the males of its species within reach of the net.

In the frontispiece I give an illustration showing the names of the various parts of a butterfly's wings as used in Col. Bingham's work.

For assistance in writing these notes I am much indebted to the following:— To the Hon. Mr. F. M. Mackwood, who has for over 30 years always given me the benefit of his experience, and has been very liberal in supplying me with varieties. To Capt. Norman D. Riley of the British Museum (Natural History) for reading the manuscript, and giving me all the help in his power in bringing the nomenclature up-to-date, and identifying several species for me. To Lt.-Col. W. H. Evans, R.E., Mr. T. R. Bell, I.F.S. (retired), Mr. T. Bainbrigge-Fletcher, Indian Imperial Entomologist, and the late Mr. F. Hannyngton, I.C.S., for sending me numerous Indian specimens, and other assistance; to Mr. J.J. Joicey for lending me Messrs. Elwes and Edward's original dissections of *Hesperiidæ*, and many specimens, and to Mr. G. M. Henry, of the Colombo Museum, who has made most of the sketches for the coloured plates, and helped me in many ways.

W. O.

THE

BUTTERFLIES OF CEYLON.

NYMPHALIDÆ

Danainæ.

1. HESTIA JASONIA, De N., B., E. *Nectaria jasonia.* M. Fruhstorfer treats it as a race of the Malayan *lynceus.* Peculiar to Ceylon. It differs from *H. malabarica* of S. India in having "the black spot in the cell of the upper wing large and confluent with the black costal patch above, and the three subapical spots large and coalescing." (De N.) It is common in forests where there is a fairly heavy rainfall though occasionally specimens may be seen making long flights over the open country

The females have the wings broader in proportion to their length, and in specimens caught in the same district and season, are usually larger and lighter in colour.

It is subject to great climatic variation, specimens from the wet low country being very much smaller and darker than those from the Hills. By far the smallest and darkest series I have seen were shown to me by Mr. F. M. Mackwood; they were caught at Badura Eliya in the Kalutara district in July (wet season). The fore wing of an average male from Haputale measured 100×35 m.m. while that of an average male from Galle measured 62×27 m.m. These two specimens are in the British Museum collection.

It is found from sea level to an elevation of 5,000 feet at least, but I have never noticed it in the North or Eastern parts of the Island. It is fond of flying high but, when in reach, it is very easy to catch as it has a slow hovering flight.

2. DANAIDA (RADENA) EXPROMPTA, M., De N. *Radena vulgaris exprompta* B. *Radena similis exprompta* E.

Peculiar to Ceylon and only found in the South West of the Island. It is allied to *D. vulgaris* which is found in Burmah and Malaya. De Nicéville writes: "The true *D. similis*, which is a native of China and Formosa only really differs from *D. vulgaris* in being somewhat larger." *D. vulgaris* is not found in India, west of Burmah, but it seems to have thrown off races to Ceylon and the Nicobar Islands (*exprompta* and *nicobarica*). De Nicéville distinguishes these races from *vulgaris* as follows :—

a. The white streaks from the base narrow ; no defined black border to wings=*vulgaris.*

b. The whitish spaces on the basal area greatly predominating, leaving a well defined black border beyond = *exprompta* and *nicobarica.*

It is so constant and well defined a form, and so well separated geographically, that it seems to deserve specific rank. It bears a superficial resemblance to *D. aglea* but can be easily distinguished on the wing by the browner colour of the under side, which is rendered conspicuous by its manner of flight, and by having the cell of the fore-wing crossed vertically by a broad black band. The male has no sex mark but has slightly narrower and less rounded wings than the female.

It is common in the Galle district, being especially abundant at Kottawa early in the year. I have also noted it at Bentota and Tebuwana.

3. DANAIDA (TIRUMALA) LIMNIACE.

Fruhstorfer names the Ceylon race *mutina.*

Also found in India, Burmah and S. China.

A very common low country insect, but it is found at all elevations during, and shortly after, the flights. It has a fairly strong flight while migrating but, at other times, it flies slowly and settles frequently on flowers or wet patches on the roads. It may be taken all the year round but is most plentiful during the NE. monsoon.

4. DANAIDA (TIRUMALA) SEPTENTRIONIS. M., De N., B. *Danais (Tirumala) melissa musikanos E.*

Two forms of *septentrionis* are found in India ; one from Tenasserim, Assam, and the Eastern Himalayas, and the other from S. India. The latter differs from the Northern form in being much smaller, and in its "much lighter general tone of colouration" (De N.). Bingham and De Nicéville agree in uniting them as *septentrionis*, but Fruhstorfer has separated them as races of *melissa* which is found in Java. He names the North Indian form *septentrionis,* that from South India—*dravidarum,* and our Ceylon form, which is intermediate in colour between them, *musikanos.* Material in the British Museum is insufficient to prove whether our form can be separated from those of India.

It occurs in the same places, and at the same times as *limniace,* but is far more numerous. It usually shares with *Euplœa asela* the honour of starting the NE. monsoon flights. Its flight while migrating is much slower than that of *limniace,* and it is not addicted to settling on wet roads; otherwise its habits are similar.

Occasionally, during the flights, hundreds of their wings may be found in places along the roads. I believe this to be mainly the work of the White-bellied Drongo (*Dicrurus leucopygialis*), as I have watched this bird catching them, eating the body, and dropping the wings. I have also seen the blood-sucker lizard (*Calotes sp.*) eating them.

It is found everywhere in the Island all the year round but is most abundant during the NE. monsoon.

5. Danaida (Salatura) chrysippus.

Found in Europe, Africa and Southern Asia.

The most sedentary of all the Ceylon Danaids; it may be found day after day in the same place, if disturbed it flies off but soon returns. It apparently does not join in the flights.

Specimens from Haldummulla are usually much smaller than those from the low-country, although the food plant is very abundant here. It is found all over the Island all the year round. It is slightly variable, and Mr. A. C. Hayley has shown me a series, bred at Galle, in which the white marginal spots on the hind wing are obsolete.

Var. *dorippus.* In this the black apical patch and the white sub-apical band on the fore wing are wanting. It is very rare, the only specimens I have seen till recently being four in the Colombo Museum collection. I have now received one from Giants Tank, Mannar district. It is common in Africa.

Var. *alcippus.* In this the lower wings are suffused with white. There are two specimens in the Colombo Museum but I have seen no others I have a female which shows a tendency to approach this form, veins 2, 3, 4 and 5, on the upper side of the hind wing, being narrowly edged with white.

6. Danaida (Salatura) plexippus, B., E.; *Salatura genutia*, M., De N.

Found in India, Burmah, Malaya, S. China, etc.

Bell says ("Common Butterflies of the Plains of India"): "Some specimens from dry regions show a tendency to replace the tawny part of the hind wing by white, thus approaching the next species" (*D. hegesippus*). I have noticed this variation, to a slight extent, occasionally in Ceylon, but it is not here confined to the dry zone, as I have found it most frequently at Galle and Haldummulla. In Ceylon, however, the dry regions have been, so far, very little worked and little is known of the variations to be found there.

It is a much more active insect than the last, and joins to a limited extent in the flights. It is common all over the Island all the year round.

7. Danaida (Parantica) aglea, B., E.; *Parantica ceylonica*, M.; *Danais ceylanica*, De N.

De Nicéville says: "*D. ceylanica* is really a local form of *D. grammica*, which is the common S. Indian species...... it is doubtful whether the name *ceylanica* should not be suppressed and the Ceylon species be included under the name *grammica*." He gives *D. aglea* as the form from N. India and Burmah. Bingham gives *aglea* as the S. Indian and Ceylon form, and *melanoides* as that from Northern and Eastern India; it differs in having the wings longer and narrower, and the hyaline marks very much broader than in *aglea*.

Ceylon specimens vary in the width of the hyaline marks.

It is very plentiful at all elevations in the southern half of the Island all the year round, but especially so during the NE. monsoon. It becomes scarcer in the north and I have so far no notes of its capture in Jaffna and Mannar. It joins to a very limited extent in the flights.

8. Danaida (Chittira) fumata, M., B., E. *Chittira taprobana*, De N.

Peculiar to Ceylon and confined to high elevations, where

it is extremely abundant all the year round. It flies very slowly and settles frequently on flowers, so is very easy to catch. It does not join in the flights.

It is extremely abundant at Nuwara Eliya, Patipola, the Horton Plains, etc., and is not rare in wet weather at Haldummulla. I have never personally seen a specimen below approximately 3,000 feet elevation.

The larva feeds on *Allæophania decipiens* ("Spolia Zeylanica," Vol. X., Part XXXVI.).

9. EUPLŒA (CRASTIA) CORE ASELA, B., E.; *Euplœa asela*, M., De N.

"More or less confined to Ceylon though incidentally recorded from Western India" (Bingham). It is a race of *core* from which it differs in having the terminal and subterminal spots on the fore wing smaller and duller in colour, These spots are very variable in Ceylon specimens; in my series they vary from 3 to 21 in number; in the latter specimen those at the apex are very large and diffuse. They are, however, always very dull white or buff, and never as bright as in the specimens of *core* that I have seen.

It is very common all the year round everywhere, but is particularly abundant in the flights. It settles readily at flowers, particularly *Gynura ceylanica* and a species of wild heliotrope; and I have frequently seen it in clusters, apparently feeding, at an exposed root or dead stick.

The larvæ feed on Oleander, Ficus, etc.

10. EUPLŒA CORUS, B. E.; *Macroplœa elisa*, M., De N.

Peculiar to Ceylon and confined to the South West littoral tracts. The furthest inland I have seen it is at Kottawa, ten miles from Galle.

It is said to have been formerly common at Colombo and Galle, but owing to building and cultivation it is getting scarce there, and a perfect specimen is quite a prize.

Its flight is slow and it settles often, so it is very easy to catch.

11. EUPLŒA (SALPINX) KOLLARI SINHALA, B.; *Isamia sinhala*, M.; *Salpinx sinhala*, De N.; *Salpinx klugii sinhala*, E,

Peculiar to Ceylon, but is only an insular race of *E. kollari* of India from which it differs in the same way that *asela* differs from *core*. It varies in the number and size of the spots. *E. kollari* is regarded by some authors as only a race of *klugii*.

A common insect in the drier low-country. It often joins in the flights, and in December, 1902, it was for a few days by far the commonest *Euplœa* in the flight.

It is very common at Wellawaya, in the low-country of Uva, and at Anuradhapura. I have also taken it at Galle and Jaffna.

It is not found at high elevations, except during the flights.

12. EUPLŒA (STICTOPLŒA) CORETA MONTANA, B., E.; *Naramada montana*, M. *Stictoplœa montana*, De N.—Peculiar to Ceylon, but is only a race of the Indian *E. coreta*, from which it differs in the same way as *asela* from *core* and *sinhala* from *kollari*

It is almost as abundant as *asela* in the flights, but does not usually appear till they have been on for some days.

Like *sinhala*, it does not seem to remain at high elevations after the flights end; but it is then common in many parts of the low-country, particularly in the dry zone.

The females of the three species *asela*, *sinhala*, and *montana* are difficult to distinguish. The usual rule is—

A.—Under side fore wing : no spot in cell = *sinhala*.

B.—Under side fore wing : white spot in cell :

A 1.—No spots outside cell in interspaces 5 and 6 = *asela*.

B 1.—Complete series of spots between veins immediately outside cell = *montana*.

I have specimens of both *asela* and *montana* without the spot in the cell. This variety is quite common. I have also—

montana : Only 4 spots outside cell ; no spot in interspace 5.

asela : 6 spots outside cell ; spot in interspace 6.

In my series of *montana*, the spots outside cell vary from

4 to 7. In *asela* from 3 to 6.

Mr. A. C. Hayley has called my attention to another means of distinguishing them, which, to judge from the specimens in my collection, seems reliable.

In interspace 1 on the under side of the fore wing—

♀ *asela* has one long milky white streak (about 10 mm. long).

♀ *montana* has two similar streaks.

♀ *sinhala* has a very minute white streak, or narrow spot, seldom over 2 mm. in length.

The males can be easily distinguished by the sex mark, which is a black shiny mark in interspace 1 of the upper side of the fore wing, as follows :—

One short narrow streak = *asela*.

Two long rather broad streaks = *montana*.

One short oval spot = *sinhala*.

SATYRINÆ.

13. ORSOTRIOENA MANDATA, M., De N.; *Orsotrioena meda mandata*, B., E.

Found also in S. India.

It is so constant and geographically separated a form that it seems to deserve specific rank, though the more recent writers treat it as a race of *O. meda* of N. India, Burmah, Malaya, etc., from which it differs " on the under side in having the transverse band three times the width that it is in that species " (Moore). It varies very little in Ceylon, but I have seen two specimens in which the white band was almost obsolete. One was taken by Mr. T. G. Elliott at Kumbukkan, near Moneragalla, and the other by Mr. John Pole at Nawalapitiya. The latter is figured in "Spolia Zeylanica," Vol. IX., Part XXXIII. They are however quite distinct from *meda*.

It is very common all over the southern portion of the Island, from sea level to over 4,000 feet at least, all the year round, but I have not yet noted it in the Northern or North-Central Provinces. It is found in paddy-fields and in grass by the roadsides, or near jungle, but does not usually frequent the patanas away from jungle. It sometimes comes to toddy or sugar.

14. MYCALESIS (CALYSISME) PERSEUS TYPHLUS, E. *Calysisme perseus*, M., De N., B. Moore also gives *blasius* which is the wet season form. Evans separates *typhlus* as the Indian and Ceylon race, restricting *perseus* to Kangra and Burma. It is smaller than *perseus*, and the ocellus on the fore wing is usually absent in the wet season form.

It varies very greatly in the number and size of the ocelli both on the upper and under surfaces, and some specimens are difficult to separate from the next species (*M. polydecta*).

It is very common at Haldummulla, on grass by the roadsides, or on patanas, and I have found it equally plentiful at Elpitiya, in the Southern Province, on patana, very little above sea level. I have also taken it at Galle and from 500 to over 5,000 feet in Uva. I have never seen it in the Northern Province. The wet and dry season forms usually fly together. It comes to sugar occasionally.

15. MYCALESIS (CALYSISME) MINEUS POLYDECTA, B., E. *Calysisme mineus*, M., De N.

Also found in India. Bingham says: "There are no constant characters by which this race may be distinguished from *M. mineus*." De Nicéville gives *polydecta* from Burmah, Sumatra and Celebes and says: " It is doubtful whether this species really occurs in India," but in a small pamphlet published by the late Col. Manders and De Nicéville on Ceylon butterflies, he revises this opinion and gives our form as *polydecta*.

It is extremely variable in every respect, and some varieties are difficult to distinguish from *M. typhlus*. Those taken on patanas in Uva from 500 to 2,000 feet elevation are usually larger and much more conspicuously marked than those from higher elevations.

It is very plentiful in Uva, on patanas or on grass by the roadsides. I have taken it also at Galle but it is very rare there. It is easy to breed as the females lay eggs freely in captivity

16. MYCALESIS (CALYSISME) SUBDITA, B., E.

Also found in S. India. It is not mentioned by Moore or De Nicéville as it apparently only differs from *polydecta* in having the sex mark of the male much larger and paler, and this was not regarded as a distinguishing mark when the " Lepidoptera of Ceylon " and "The Butterflies of India, etc.," were published.

Common on the roadsides at Haldummulla, especially in May, June, and July, but I have not yet taken it above 3,000 feet.

It is the only Mycalesis I have taken in the Northern Province. It is common at Anuradhapura, and occurs sparingly in the Jaffna Peninsula. Rare at Galle.

It seems to come to sugar more readily than *typhlus* or *polydecta*, and is very easy to breed.

" Kandy and Ratnapura " (F. M Mackwood).

The last three species are exceedingly variable and difficult to distinguish. The males of *typhlus* and *polydecta* have a small dark brown sex mark near the dorsal margin of the under side of the fore wing; *subdita* has a much larger ochreous one Bingham discriminates the two former by hind wing under side :—

Posterior *three* ocelli only in a straight line = *typhlus*.

Posterior *four* ocelli straight = *polydecta*.

From my specimens this does not seem entirely reliable, as I have very typical *polydecta* in which the last four ocelli are not straight, though not so much out of line as in typical *typhlus*.

Personally I know no rule by which I can separate the two with certainty, as they grade almost perfectly into one another. *M. subdita* has a far larger and lighter sex mark than either, but the female is, so far as I can see, quite indistinguishable from *polydecta* ♀. The marginal lines on the upper side are perhaps a little clearer.

The breeding experiments I have carried out so far are quite inconclusive. Being bred where the female was caught, they have, as was to be expected, bred fairly true. The very small number of collectors in the Island prohibits experiments being carried out on a large enough scale to settle the question.

17. MYCALESIS (CALYSISME) RAMA, E.; *Calysisme drusia*, M.—Peculiar to Ceylon, and only found in the wet zone. Moore describes *drusia* from a single specimen taken in the Kottawa forest. *M. rama* has been taken there, and Moore's description agrees fairly well with it.

I procured specimens of the dry season form from Ratnapura in March, 1917. It differs in having the ocelli and other markings on the under side more or less obsolescent and the ground colour paler. The upper side is almost identical with that of the wet season form in both sexes.

Till recently it was only known from specimens taken at Udagama (near Kottawa) by the late Mr. John Pole. It has now been discovered to be quite common in bamboo jungle at Ratnapura.

I have never taken it personally, but have specimens given to me by Mr. Mackwood from Ratnapura, and some caught by a native collector at Kottawa.

It can be distinguished at once by the colour of the under side, which is *ochreous* brown, viz., far more yellow than in any other Ceylon *Mycalesis*.

18. NISSANGA PATNIA, M. *Mycalesis* (*Nissanga*) *patnia*, E. The genitalia of this species differ so widely from those of *Mycalesis* in Ceylon, that I keep it in a separate genus.

It shows considerable seasonal variation and very dark forms may be taken in the wettest districts. I have a fine series of them from Kandy, taken in June, July and August, and specimens from Deniyaya.

It frequents jungle or shady roadsides and swarms on the fallen fruit of Ficus and other trees. It also comes readily to toddy, or sugar, but is easily alarmed.

It is very common at Haldummulla all the year round, and in the South, at Galle and other places, but I have not yet come across it in the Northern Province.

19. LETHE (HANIPHA) DYNSATE, M.; *Lethe* (*Debis*) *dynsate*, E.

Peculiar to Ceylon and a great rarity. Moore separates the variety from the Hills as *H. sinhala:* he says the female differs from female *dynsate* as follows: Narrower discal band on fore wing, more defined apical white and black spots on fore wing, under side fore wing has five sub-marginal spots instead of four, hind wing has all the spots smaller. He does not describe the male of the Hill form. From the limited material at my disposal I would say that both sexes of the Hill form differ from Ratnapura specimens in having the ocelli on the under side of the hind wing very minute; the discal white band on the fore wing of the female is also much narrower.

I have no personal experience of the habits of the low-country form as I owe my specimens to Mr. Mackwood's generosity, but I have seen a fair number of the males of the Hill form in the jungles from Haputale to Ohiya, and the Horton Plains. On a fine morning they fly rapidly round the tree tops, usually settling high up. Occasionally they descend within reach, and a very quick stroke will catch them. Unfortunately their wings are very fragile, and the stroke must be quick, so I have damaged all I have caught.

I have tried sugaring for them without result so far but I am confident that they will come if I can find the right bait, or time of day.

20. LETHE DRYPETIS, M., De N., B.; *Lethe drypetis todara*, E

According to Moore *drypetis* from Ceylon differs from *todara* of S. India by having, in the male, " three submarginal very indistinct small black spots " on the upper side of the hind wing, and, in the female, the white discal band on the fore wing is " macular," while in *todara* it is " irregular." The discal band in the female varies in Ceylon; usually it could not be rightly described as "macular," but in some specimens, taken during the wet season at Kandy, it shows a tendency to break up into three spots and Moore evidently described *drypetis* from one of this type. De Nicéville says:

"We can detect not the slightest difference between the Ceylon and continental examples," and Bingham ignores *todara*. Apparently therefore *todara* is only a slight seasonal variety of *drypetis*.

It may be found in all bamboo jungle where there is a fairly large rainfall, from sea level to 7,000 feet elevation at least. It is very common at Haputale and Kandy nearly all the year round, and I have also noted it at Galle, Ratnapura, Ohiya, etc. It comes readily to toddy or sugar.

21. LETHE DYRTA NILGIRIENSIS, E.; *Lethe neelgheriensis*, M., De N.; *Lethe rohria nilgiriensis*, B.

Also found in S. India.

Fruhstorfer separates the Ceylon race as *yoga*.

De Nicéville considers it "notably distinct" from *L. dyrta*.

The male differs from the male *rohria* in having a fourth white spot on the upper side of the fore wing, in interspace 2. I have two specimens, taken at Kandy and Haldummulla respectively, in which this spot is practically obsolete, and one specimen which shows a minute fifth spot in interspace 3

The female differs in having the white pre-apical band on the fore wing broken up into three white spots. I have noticed no tendency in these spots to unite and form a band.

The larva feeds on grasses; the butterfly is very common at Haldummulla in grass-fields and chenas, and is very easy to catch, as it only flies a very short distance at a time. It comes occasionally to sugar.

Taken from 1,000 to 5,000 feet elevation in Uva, but I have no notes of its capture out of the Province, except the one specimen from Kandy. I believe it to be common everywhere in the hills. Flies all the year round.

22. LETHE DARETIS.—Peculiar to Ceylon, and confined to high elevations. Personally I have never taken it below 4,500 feet.

It is nearly always to be found settled on the banks where the earth has been cut away to make a road, and never far from a bamboo clump.

If disturbed, it flies away rapidly, but soon settles again Its wings are very fragile, and it is easily damaged by the net. It comes readily to toddy, etc.

February and August are, in my experience, the best months for fresh-hatched specimens, but a few may be taken all the year round.

Localities: Nuwara Eliya, Horton Plains, Ohiya, etc.

23. YPTHIMA SINGALA, M., De N., *Ypthima avanta singala*, B. *Ypthima (Thymipa) avanta singala*, E.

Also found in India.

Y. avanta is found in the Western Himalayas and Burmah. It differs from *singala* in having a sex mark on the fore wing of the male, and very conspicuous transverse dark fasciæ on the under side.

Moore also gives *Y. thora*, but it is certainly only a variety. It differs only in having a minute sub-apical bi-pupilled ocellus on the upper side of the fore wing of the male.

The number of ocelli on the under side of the hind wing varies in my specimens from 4 to 7, and is not always the same on both wings. They also vary as much in size as in number; but this does not seem to depend on season or climate, except that I have only taken a variety with the ocelli reduced to mere specks at the highest elevations.

Specimens from Elpitiya, near Galle, taken during the rains, agree very well with those taken at Haldummulla during the drought, except that var. *thora* was proportionately more abundant at the lower elevation.

Common all over the Uva patanas from 500 to over 5,000 feet; Galaha, near Kandy; and Elpitiya, near Galle. Flies all the year round at Haldummulla.

24. YPTHIMA CEYLONICA, M., De N., E.; *Ypthima huebneri ceylonica*, B.

Also found in S. India.

Y. huebneri, which is found in India, Burmah, Malaya, etc., differs in having the whole of the upper side of the hind wing brown. De Nicéville says of *ceylonica* that: "In the Orissa specimens the striation of the "under sides is denser, and shows a considerable approximation to *Y. huebneri*, to which it is evidently closely allied." Elwes has found that the genitalia differ from those of *huebneri*.

It is common everywhere all the year round, especially along roadsides. The variation in the size of the ocelli in this species seems largely to depend on temperature. I have taken specimens with exceptionally large ocelli at Kottawa (wet zone) and Jaffna (dry zone). They vary slightly, according to the season, at Haldummulla, being rather smaller in the dry season.

I have seen swallows eating them. I have a variety of the female in which the ground colour is very pale ochreous brown.

25. MELANITIS LEDA. *Melanitis ismene*, M., B., De N.—*Melanitis leda ismene*, E.

Also found in Africa, Asia and Australia. *Leda* is an older name than *ismene*.

Bingham says *ismene* is the dry, and *leda* the wet season form. Both forms are extremely variable, and seem to grade perfectly. I have found *leda* commonest in growing paddy, but elsewhere varieties of *ismene* are usually far more abundant. It is found all over the Island, but all I have taken in the extreme North were *ismene*.

It flies very little in the daytime but starts at dusk, when it has a very jerky, and fairly rapid flight, and is not easy to catch. The bad light, of course, is against success. It comes readily to sugar after dark till, at any rate, 9 p.m. It also comes in the daytime in shady places, but is very shy then.

26. MELANITIS PHEDIMA TAMBRA, E. *Melanitis bela tambra*, B. *Melanitis tambra*, M., De N.

Phedima is an older name than *bela*. Peculiar to Ceylon.

There are two very distinct forms: 1st. Upper side deep dusky brown with the outer margin of the fore wing nearly straight and 2nd. Upper side reddish brown with the outer margin strongly falcated. They vary much less than *ismene* and do not grade into one another. Moore describes the black form as the male, and the red one as the female and the series in the British Museum collection, and in my own, bear this out. Some writers have treated them as seasonal forms of *tambra*, but De Nicéville described the black form as *M. aswa* var. *suyudana.* I have so far failed to get the female to lay eggs in captivity.

The black form is seldom seen out of jungle, where it settles in the heaviest undergrowth, but the red one is common in cultivated land, and seems to be particularly fond of the shade of jak trees, and its under side, when settled, matches the dead leaves well. In habits otherwise they are similar to *leda*, flying little by day, but coming out at dusk, and coming readily to sugar after dark.

I have specimens from Haldummulla, Kandy, Ratnapura and Kottawa.

27. Elymnias hypermnestra fraterna, E. *Elymnias undularis fraterna*, B.; *Elymnias fraterna*, M.; *Elymnias undularis* var. *fraterna*, De N., E.

Peculiar to Ceylon but is a race or variety of *hypermnestra*, from India, Burmah and Java. *Hypermnestra* is an older name than *undularis*.

De Nicéville says: "*E. fraterna* is nothing more than a local variety of *E. undularis;* the females are indistinguishable but the males have the ferruginous border of the hind wing narrower and brighter, and scarcely any trace of the bluish marks on the fore wing, the under side is also paler."

Bingham says the ♂ differs in having the terminal margin of hind wing ochraceous, not chestnut. ♀ has the oblique pre-apical white band on fore wing narrow, its margins even.

The males in Ceylon are extremely variable. In those in my collection the width of the ferruginous band, taken at the widest spot, viz., vein 4, varies from 6 to 10 mm. In one the fore wing is entirely blackish-brown, with no trace of blue. In a second the colour is the same, with three very conspicuous elongated sub-apical blue spots. In a third there is a terminal marginal border of ferruginous, narrowing from the apex to the tornus, and two faint sub-apical blue treaks. In a fourth there is a complete row of sub-terminal blue spots, much elongated at the apex, thus approaching very near to *undularis*, but the terminal border on the hind wing is exceptionally pale and wide, and has white sub-terminal spots in interspaces 2, 3, and 4.

The female varies much in the width of the sub-apical white band.

The flight is slow, and it always settles low down, though very seldom actually on the ground. The female is a mimic of *D. plexippus*. In most cases of mimicry in Ceylon an experienced collector can usually distinguish the mimic by its different flight. *E. fraterna*, however, is far better as a mimic on the wing than in the cabinet, and very frequently deceives me. Possibly this may be due to the fact that it usually flies low, and is seen from above as a bird would probably see it. If seen from below the under side would, of course, destroy the illusion.

Rare at Haldummulla, but very common in the coconut districts, especially where the palms are low, in new clearings, etc. The larvæ and pupæ may often be found on pot palms in low-country verandahs.

27A. ELYMNIAS MERULA.—Colonel Swinhoe gives this as a new species from Ceylon (Ann. Mag. Nat. Hist., No. 93, September, 1915, Vol. XVI., page 171). His description is: "♂ upper side deep black, as dark as *E. hecate*, Butler, from North Borneo; fore wing with the costa spotted with blue, three blue streaks near the apex, and three sub-marginal blue spots in interspaces 2, 3, and 4; hind wing with a slight shade of fulvous on the outer margin; outer margins of both wings as in *hecate*. Under side dark chestnut-brown, densely striated with pale blue, fore wing with white costal points, which become thickly clustered together at the apex; hind wing with a small bluish-white spot below the middle of the costa

"Expanse of wing, 2 $\frac{8}{10}$ inches

"Habitat: Kandy, Ceylon.

"Except for the white spot on the hind wings beneath, it much resembles *hecate*."

I know nothing of the history of this insect. It is difficult to imagine a new species of a large butterfly being discovered at Kandy, which is the headquarters of the native collectors and the best worked district in Ceylon. From the description it seems possible that it may be a melanism of *E. fraterna*. It is larger than normal in that species, but the description of the under side tallies very closely.

28. Elymnias singhala, M. and B.; *Dyctis singhala*, De N.; *Elymnias* (*Melynias*) *singhala*, E

Peculiar to Ceylon.

Peradeniya is the headquarters of this insect, but it occurs sparingly in widely scattered localities. I have caught four specimens only at Haldummulla, two in 1889, when I was starting my Ceylon collection, and therefore catching everything, and one each in November of 1914 and 1915.

It is very like a *Euplœa* on the wing, and so, I believe, often escapes notice. It is very easy to catch when identified.

It is rare in the Kottawa forest, and has been taken at Ratnapura.

MORPHINÆ.

29. Discophora lepida.—Also found in Southern India.

Fruhstorfer separates our race as *ceylonica*.

The male varies much in the number and size of the ocelli on the under side of the hind wing. I have one specimen with five perfectly formed and fairly large ocelli.

A great rarity till its habits became known; the male is now easily obtainable, but the female is a prize.

The male flies all the year round, but does not appear till dusk. It has its particular haunts, and a few may be found there any evening, flying backwards and forwards, with a very jerky and rather fast flight. Thanks to the bad light, they are then difficult to catch. I have searched frequently in a small jungle where I knew there were plenty, but have never succeeded in putting up a male in the daytime. The only two females I have seen on the wing were both flying in the middle of the day. The ♂ comes readily to sugar as soon as it is dark; the ♀ is said to come in the daytime (especially to overripe jak fruit), but is very shy. Possibly, like *M. leda*, both would come better at night, and be easier to catch. Personally I have not yet tried sugaring for them after 7 p.m.

Bell says the females come to meet the males in their evening flight, and thinks they are attracted by the strong scent the males are notorious for He describes the scent as that of a mixture of apples and lemons. ("Common Butterflies of the Plains of India.") If this is so, the females might be caught by enclosing a few males in a muslin cage, and watching near, preferably after dark.

A well-known haunt of the males is behind Kottawa rest-house, where the stream leaves the jungle.

Common at Galle, Ratnapura, Balangoda, Avissawella, and probably in all bamboo jungle in the south-west of the Island.

NYMPHALINÆ.

30. Charaxes (Haridra) psaphon.

Moore describes the female as *H. serendiba*.

It is confined to Ceylon, but is closely allied to *C. imna* of S. India. De Nicéville distinguishes them as follows:—"Black border of male on hind wing very broad at costa, continuous = *psaphon*. Black border of male on hind wing less broad, decreasing to distinct spots towards anal angle = *imna*." He says that S. Indian specimens of *imna* approximate very closely to *psaphon*, but further north the divergence increases. Ceylon specimens also vary considerably in the width of this band, and in its continuation to the anal angle.

It is not at all a rare insect in the low-country, but it is usually difficult to capture. The male is often seen sitting on wet patches on the roads, and comes readily to sugar or toddy. It is rather shy when settled on the roads, but I once caught six drinking at one patch of sap exuding from a tree, and it was not easy to drive them off. The females also come to sugar occasionally, but are very shy and difficult to approach.

The female is seen up-country far more often than the male, but it is then nearly always flying very fast; it seldom seems to settle, and is almost impossible to catch. The greatest elevation at which I have seen it is at Haputale, 4,800 feet.

It is most plentiful in Uva during the SW. monsoon, but it is not rare in March and April.

31. CHARAXES FABIUS.—Fruhstorfer calls the Ceylon race *cerynthus*.

Also found in India and Burmah.

The ♀♀ have much longer tails than the ♂♂

The habits of the males are very much like those of male *psaphon*. They are frequently seen on the wet roads in the low-country of Uva, and come readily to sugar or toddy. The females apparently do not 'flight' at high elevations like female *psaphon*, but I have seen a specimen taken at Nakiadeniya, near Galle, which is a very long way from its usual haunts.

It may be taken in the dry low-country all the year round and I have noticed it at Anuradhapura, Trincomalie, and Jaffna. It is very rare at Haldummulla but abundant at Wellawaya.

32. EULEPIS ATHAMAS AGRARIUS, E.; *Eulepis athamas*, B., De N.; *Eulepis samatha*, M.

E. athamas is found all over India and Burmah. Messrs. Rothschild and Jordan separate *agrarius* as a race occurring in S. India and Ceylon. *E. samatha* and *agrarius* differ mainly from *athamas* in being smaller and having the greenish yellow band narrower. De Nicéville writes: "The only conclusion I can come to after a patient examination of all the facts, in conjunction with a very large series of specimens from nearly every part of India, is that there is but one species, *C. athamas*, which is variable in all the characters which have been taken by different writers in describing the many species which are said to be allied to, but different from, the parent species, and that these variations are not confined to any particular geographical range of country, nor are they constant."

It varies in Ceylon in the width of the yellow band and the size of the pre-apical spots.

It may be found day after day in the same place there is one spot on Kalupahani Estate where I can be almost certain to see it on every fine day for nine months of the year. It settles high up on a leaf, and flies round very fast, often returning to the same leaf, and is very difficult to catch. It comes well to toddy in the dry low-country, but very rarely at Haldummulla. It may also be taken at carrion. The females are seldom caught in good condition, but I have watched them laying their eggs on Albizzia Moluccana here.

It is found from sea level up to 5,000 feet at least, and I have taken it at Haputale, Kegalle, Trincomalie, etc.

33. APATURA (ROHANA) PARISATIS CAMIBA, E., B.; *Rohana Camiba*, M., De N.

A. parisatis is found in N. India, Burmah, S. China, etc., the race *camiba* is confined to S. India and Ceylon. It differs from *parisatis* mainly in the number of the minute pre-apical white spots in both sexes. In the male, *camiba* has 3 spots, *parisatis* only one. In the female, *camiba* has 4 or 5 spots, *parisatis* has usually 3. About half the specimens of male *camiba* in my collection have 4 white spots, but the fourth is very minute, and might easily escape notice. The females are extremely variable in colour and clearness of markings.

The male is common and easy to capture. The female is much scarcer, and is usually found in jungle; it is very hard to catch in good condition.

It is found from sea level to 6,000 feet at least, and is common at Haldummulla and Kandy, and I have specimens from Trincomalie, Ohiya, Kegalle, etc., but none from Galle or the extreme North.

34. PARTHENOS CYANEUS, M. and De N.; *Parthenos virens cyaneus*, B.; *Parthenos gambrisius cyaneus*, E.

Peculiar to Ceylon. It varies very little. It is very distinct in colour from *gambrisius* or *virens*; *gambrisius* is described as "greenish olivaceous," and *virens* as "light brassy green " (De N.). There are also constant differences in the markings, and it seems to deserve specific rank.

Above 2,500 feet it seems rarely to settle, but is always seen flying fast and straight across country. In the low-country its behaviour is quite different; it is usually found in jungle and settles high up in the trees, going off occasionally for a rapid fly round, but nearly always returning to the same spot. From this I fancy that the up-country specimens are probably all females searching for new breeding grounds. Unfortunately they are very hard to catch, so I cannot be certain.

Occurs at Haldummulla all the year round. In December and January the high wind sometimes forces them to settle in the tea, and they are then easy to catch.

I have taken them on the Horton Plains (7,200 feet), and at Haputale (5,000 feet), Wellawaya (600 feet), Ratnapura, Kottawa, and Kegalla, and believe they are common wherever there is a fair rainfall.

35. EUTHALIA NAIS, B., E.; *Symphaedra nais*, M., De N.—Also found in Southern India and the Himalayas. *See* Plate I., fig. 1.

Very variable in the amount of black on the upper side and white below.

Very unlike the other *Euthalias* in Ceylon, both in appearance and habits, except that both sexes come readily to toddy The latter are far more like those of a *Precis*. It almost invariably settles on the ground, and if disturbed, flies very quickly for a short distance, returning to the original spot, usually in a few minutes. Very rarely individuals seem to be afflicted with the migrating mania, and may be met a few miles from their haunts, flying very fast and straight. These sometimes settle, but if disturbed go on straight away. I have noticed them in March and August on this estate, going straight in the direction of Adam's Peak. If these are efforts to find new breeding grounds, they do not appear to be very successful. They are, so far as I am aware, only common in one very limited area in Ceylon, viz., a stretch of quartzy patana, reaching from Ranungahawa, four miles below Haldummulla, to Kumbukkan (25 to 30 miles). This patana crosses the Wellawaya-Haldummulla road near the 127th milepost: the butterfly can nearly always be taken there. I have found it abundant there in March, May and August, and at other parts of the patana in July and November.

36. EUTHALIA (DOPHLA) EVELINA.

Peculiar to Ceylon, but a race of it, *E. evelina laudabilis*, is found in S. India. It differs in having a greyish white band along the costa of the fore wing.

Occasionally very common in parts of the low-country of Uva, but very rarely comes above 2,000 feet. It is fond of settling in wet sand on the river-beds, or where sap is exuding from a tree, and both sexes come very readily to toddy.

The largest numbers I have ever seen were at Hambegama Tank in June. It is not rare at Wellawaya, and I have taken it once at Haldummulla, 2,500 feet. Very plentiful at the hot springs near Trincomalie in November, but all were badly worn.

37. EUTHALIA LUBENTINA. Also found in India, Burma, Malaya, China, etc.

The Ceylon race is now said by Fruhstorfer to be distinct, and has been named *psittacus*.

The larva feeds on *Loranthus*, and the insect is nearly as widely distributed as the food plant, but it seems to be common nowhere. I have taken it on fallen nutmegs near Galle, in sandy river-beds in the low-country of Uva, on a Duranta hedge in my garden (3,000 feet), and in jungle above Haputale (over 5,000 feet). I have specimens from Kandy and Ratnapura, and know of its capture at Badulla.

The sexes seem to occur in about equal numbers, and both come to sugar, or settle on wet sand. In this latter characteristic the *Euthalias* differ from the majority of Ceylon butterflies, as, in other genera, those settling on wet roads or in sandy river-beds are almost invariably males. *Appias*, *Catopsilia*, and *Libythea* are the only others I can remember that agree with the *Euthalias* in this respect.

38. EUTHALIA GARUDA, M., B. and De. N.; *Euthalia garuda diversa*, E.

Found in India, Burmah, Malaya, etc. Fruhstorfer names the race from S. India and Ceylon *meridionalis*.

De Nicéville distinguishes between the males of *garuda* and *vasanta* as follows:—*E. garuda* has the white spots on the fore wing sharply defined, they "consist of a curved series of five kidney-shaped spots on a uniform pale brown ground." *E. vasanta* has the spots small, "often obsolescent or absent entirely," they are four in number and arranged in a straight, but oblique, series from the costa.

Bingham says *vasanta* differs in having no spots on the fore wing, and there are four males in the Colombo Museum labelled *garuda* because they show 4 discal white spots. My experience is that at least 20% of the males of *vasanta* in Ceylon shew these spots. The Hon. Mr. F. M. Mackwood, who has been collecting for over 50 years in the Island, has never seen a Ceylon specimen of female *garuda*, so I think there can be little doubt that *garuda* has no claim to a place in Ceylon lists.

38A. EUTHALIA VASANTA, M., De N. and E.; *Euthalia garuda vasanta*.

Peculiar to Ceylon. Fruhstorfer names the ♀♀ with white band absent *fulica*. I have never seen one.

The male varies as already stated under the heading of *E. garuda*. The female varies in the width of the white discal band, but it is always straight from the costa to interspace 2, and does not at all resemble that of the female *garuda*.

Both sexes are equally common, and have the same habits, They are fond of settling on wet roads, and come readily to decaying fruit or sugar. They are rather shy and have a very strong flight, so are not easy to capture in perfect condition.

I have notes of their capture at Colombo, Kandy, Kegalle, Galle, Trincomalie, Haldummulla, etc., but have not yet taken them in Jaffna, though the mango, which is a favourite food plant of the larvæ, is extensively cultivated there,

39. Moduza calidasa, M.; *Moduza calidosa*, De N.; *Moduza procris calidasa*, B., E.

Peculiar to Ceylon. De Nicéville thought it "quite distinct" from *procris* of India, Burmah, Malaya, etc. It differs in its quite different ground colour, different shape of the discal band, and the entire absence of the white spot at the end of the cell. Except for a very slight variation in the amount of red in the ground colour, I have noticed no tendency to grade into *proeris*, and think it entitled to specific rank.

It settles frequently on flowers but is extremely shy and difficult to catch. In the dry low-country it occasionally settles on wet patches in the roads.

It may be found at Haldummulla all the year round, but it is commonest during the SW. monsoon. It occurs from sea level to over 5,000 fect and I have found it common all over Uva and at Kottawa, and the native collectors get plenty at Kandy.

40. Neptis jumbah, M.; *Neptis jumbah*, B., De N.; *Neptis (Andrapana) jumbah*, E.

Also found in India and Burmah. Ceylon specimens have lately been named *nalanda* by Fruhstorfer as a separate race. De Nicéville says: "This is an exceedingly well marked and distinct species, and differs from all others in having a small round brown spot placed near the base on the under side of the hind wing on a white band."

It is extremely variable in the amount of white on the upper side, and the black shadings below, and also in the ground colour of the under side. I have one specimen in which the black markings below are quite obsolete.

It is common at Haldummulla all the year round, except during the heavy winds in January and February. It joins in the flights in large numbers, and when these are on it can be easily captured by walking it up in the tea in the early morning, as it then only flies a short distance. Later, when the sun gets hot, it flies straight and seldom settles.

It occurs from sea level to the Horton Plains, but I have not yet noticed it north of Vavuniya.

41. Neptis varmona, M. and De N.; *Neptis eurynome*, B.; *Neptis hylas varmona*, E.

De Nicéville writes: "The conclusion to which an examination of a large series of all the forms in which the discal band of the under side is distinctly defined with black bands leads me is, that they represent a single species, *N. varmona*, with *N. disrupta*, a casual aberration, and *N. swinhoei*, *N. kamarupa*, and *N. eurymene* as inconstant varieties." Fruhstorfer gives *disrupta* and *kamarupa* as the extreme wet and dry season forms respectively of the Ceylon race. The former is known from a single specimen only and is certainly only an aberration. *N. kamarupa* differs, on the under side, in the lighter ground colour and the narrower black edging to the white bands and spots. Ceylon specimens vary considerably in both these respects. An aberration or variety of *varmona* is figured in "Spolia Zeylanica," Vol. IX., Part XXXIII. In 1918 I received a similar specimen from Kandy, and in 1919 the Hon. Mr. F. M. Mackwood received two more from the same locality. It may be an extreme wet season form.

It is extremely abundant everywhere, though rather more so in the south than in the north. Freshly hatched specimens can be taken in every month of the year at Haldummulla. It does not join in the flights.

42. Rahinda hordonia sinuata, B., De N., E.; *Rahinda sinuata*, M.

Peculiar to Ceylon. It differs from *hordonia* "in the margins of the discal markings (especially the outer margins) on the upper side of the fore wing and the margins of the sub-basal and post-discal bands of the hind wing being more sinuous" (Bingham). It varies considerably in the amount of yellow on the upper side.

Very common at Haldummulla in jungles or chenas where there are plenty of thorny Acacias. It is fond of settling rather high up on these, but if disturbed only flies a short distance, so can usually be driven to a more favourable spot for capture. Especially common in May and June.

Found from 500 to over 5,000 feet elevation in Uva. I have also taken it at Madampe and Ratnapura, and believe it to be common everywhere in the hills.

43. PRECIS IPHITA, M. and De N *Junonia iphita*, B. and E. Fruhstorfer separates the race from Ceylon, S. India and the Maldives as *pluviatilis*.

Also found in India, Burma, Malaya, and China. Very abundant everywhere nearly all the year round. Appears in great numbers in the flights, especially in November-December. Except during these flights, specimens taken in the hills are usually ragged and faded. I have seen it in thousands in the sandy beds of low-country rivers, when practically every specimen appeared to be newly hatched out. From this I imagine it mainly breeds at low elevations.

Felder gives *P. intermedia* as a distinct species from Rambodde and Trincomalie. It mainly differs from typical *iphita* in showing a series of ocelli on the upper side of the fore wing. It is clearly only a variety.

44. PRECIS ATLITES. *Junonia atlites*, B., De N., E.; *Precis laomedia*, M. Also found in India, Burmah, Malaya, etc.

In habits it is very much like the last, but it is rather scarcer up-country, and even fair specimens are much harder to get in the hills. I have seen it plentiful on the sea-beach in the south, particularly at Galle in September. These all appeared to be freshly hatched. It appears up-country usually in October, before the regular flights begin, and the swarm only lasts a few days. Stragglers are fairly plentiful in November and December, but for the rest of the year they are scarce.

I have no records of its occurrence in the Northern Province, or at any very high elevation. It is extremely abundant at Kurunegala and Polgahawela in November.

45. PRECIS ORITHYIA. *Junonia orithya*, M. B.; *Junonia orithyia*, De N. and E. Found also in India, Burmah, Southern China, etc.

Fruhstorfer separates our form as *patenas*.

Does not join in the flights. It is extremely common all

the year round in the grass-fields on this estate, and all places round Haldummulla where the grass is fairly short. It is easily alarmed, and flies fast for a short distance. It never seems to fly far, but can be found in the same spots day after day. It usually settles on the ground, except when roosting for the night, when it selects a low plant about a foot or less in height. It can be walked up in the late evening, and is then very easy to catch.

It is extremely variable. Specimens from the Northern Province are much smaller than those from Haldummulla. The costa and apical markings on the fore wing are nearly pure white, whereas in the hill specimens they are pale buff; the under side also is much lighter. Specimens from the low-country of Uva taken during the dry season are intermediate between the two forms. The female is also extremely variable, at all seasons and localities, in the amount of blue on the lower wings.

Found everywhere from Galle to Jaffna, and from sea level to over 6,000 feet.

46. PRECIS HIERTA. *Junonia hierta,* De N., B., E.; *Junonia oenone*, M.

Also found in India, Burmah and S. China.

The main variation is in the size of the blue spot on the lower wing of the female. Often it is entirely absent, but in others it is as large as that of the male, but is of a more lilac shade.

From 1889 till 1916 it was seldom seen out of the Northern Province. I came across it in great numbers at Kankesanturai, on the N. coast during the NE. monsoon and took two specimens as far south as Anuradhapura. It then suddenly appeared all over the Island and I noted it at Kandy, Colombo, Galle and Tangalle. These were all perfect specimens and did not appear to have "flighted" far. They remained common in Colombo till 1919, but in 1920 the collectors there asked so exorbitant a price that I fancy they were becoming scarce again. They had quite disappeared from Kandy much earlier. These southern specimens are much larger than those from the Northern Province.

47. PRECIS LEMONIAS. *Junonia lemonias*, M., B., De N., E.

Also found in India, Burmah, Malaya, China, etc, De Nicéville says: "The under side is variable in colour, some specimens having the ground ochreous, others ferruginous, and others again beautifully pink or rosy"......"these variations are not confined to particular localities, but appear to occur indiscriminately." All varieties seem to fly together in Ceylon, but that with a bright peach-coloured under side is the rarest; I have taken it at Haldummulla.

It is occasionally very numerous at Haldummulla during the NE. monsoon flights, but in the low-country it is plentiful all the year round. It is found all over the Island, but I have not noticed it at the highest elevations.

It is particularly fond of settling on wet patches on the roads, or in the sandy river-beds.

48. PRECIS ALMANA. *Junonia almana*, De N., B., E.; *Junonia asterie*, M.

Also found in India, Burmah, Malaya, China, Japan, etc.

P. asterie is the wet season form. The dry season form is extremely rare in Ceylon, and I only possess one poor specimen, but Mr. Mackwood has shown me one or two. I found *almana* in great numbers at Giants Tank in July (dry season) but none were the dry season form.

It is abundant all over the low-country from Galle to Jaffna, especially in chenas, paddy-fields, and the borders of tanks. It is rather rare at Haldummulla, but may be taken in the grass-fields on this estate during the SW. monsoon.

49. CUPHA PLACIDA, De N., M. and B. *Cupha erymanthis placida*, E.

De Nicéville writes: "In its range it is geographically separated from *C. erymanthis*, and differs sufficiently in colouration and markings to entitle it to specific rank; but the specimens from S. India show a gradually increasing resemblance to *C. erymanthis* to the northwards of their range, very marked in some cases."

It differs from *erymanthis* as follows: "Fore-wing, discal band distinctly darker yellow, with its inner and outer margins much less sinuous and irregular, the black line defining the inner margin more slender; the spots on the band in interspaces 1, 2, and 3 much smaller, especially the spot in interspace 1, which is no larger than the others, and is diffuse and ill-defined. The sub-apical yellow spots on the black area entirely wanting, or, if present, diffuse and indistinct" (Bingham). In nearly all my specimens the spot in interspace 1 is far larger than those in 2 and 3 though not so large as in Bingham's figure of *erymanthis*.

Common wherever there is a fair rainfall. It always seems abundant at Watering Point, Galle, but is found at all elevations, and apparently all the year round. I have never seen it north of Vavuniya.

It settles on bushes usually about 5 to 8 feet from the ground. If disturbed, it dives into the thickest growth, and is therefore very difficult to capture in first-class condition.

50. CETHOSIA NIETNERI.

Peculiar to Ceylon. It usually varies little except in size, but I have seen several males from Kandy, caught in July, August, viz., the wet season, in which the ochraceous patch on the upper side is almost, or quite, obsolete.

I have records of its occurrence at Haldummulla in every month but January, but it is most numerous during the south-west monsoon.

It is one of the easiest insects to catch, owing to its slow hovering flight; its wings are not so delicate as they look, and are seldom damaged in the net.

Found all over the low-country from Galle to Vavuniya, and up to 6,000 feet (Ohiya) at least, but it seems to be most plentiful at a fair elevation, say 2,000 to 4,000 feet.

51. CYNTHIA ASELA, M., De N., and B.; *Cynthia erota asela*, E.—Peculiar to Ceylon.

"♂ absolutely indistinguishable from the wet season form of *C. erota*" (Bingham). The female differs in having the white discal band very much narrower and only extending to vein 6 on the hind wing, whereas in *erota* it extends to vein 2. The series of females in the Colombo Museum vary extremely in the width of this white band. In some it is almost obsolete on the hind wing, in others it extends to vein 5. In two of my specimens it just extends over vein 6. It also differs in the ground colour, that of *erota* from S. India being bronzy green instead of blue grey. The form with 3 ocelli on the lower wing, instead of 2, has been called *triocellata* by Fruhstorfer. The female is not very rare, but I have not yet seen a male; it is only a minor variety, and hardly worth naming.

The male is common at Haldummulla from May to August. It usually basks high up on trees, taking short flights, and returning to the same spot. It is also very frequently found settled on wet patches on the roads. It is then very easy to catch, as it is not at all shy. The female is rarer; it is usually seen flying fast and straight, but it occasionally stops at flowers. I once saw them in numbers at the blossom of *Acacia caesia*, while travelling in the coach from Polgahawella to Kegalle. I have specimens from Galle, Kandy, Wellawaya, Nuwara Eliya, etc.

52. CIRROCHROA THAIS LANKA, E.

Moore split it into *thais*, *lanka*, and *cognata*. De Nicéville gives *lanka* and *cognata*. He also mentions *swinhoei* from Ceylon but says it is not "sufficiently distinct to constitute a separate sub-species." It is very questionable whether our specimens are distinct from the S. Indian *thais*. Bingham says: "After carefully examining a long series of specimens from Southern India and Ceylon, I am quite unable to find any constant characters that would serve to distinguish *C. lanka*, Moore, from *C. thais*, Fabr." He entirely ignores *cognata* and *swinhoei*, and I personally agree with him that there is only one species in Ceylon. It is extremely variable, but all varieties seem to grade. The males can be distinguished by the different shape of the fore wing, that of the female being falcated. They also have a sex mark, the terminal half of veins 5, 6, and 7, being coloured black, with a narrow yellow margin of specialized scales.

On one occasion I was walking from Wellawaya to Koslande, in November, wet season, and on the first five miles of the road there were many thousands of the males settled on the wet patches. Both sexes often settle at flowers, but I have not found it easy to get perfect specimens of females.

It is commonest in the low-country up to 3,000 feet and I have noticed it at Haldummulla, Wellawaya, Kandy Galle, Ratnapura, Anuradhapura, Trincomalie, etc.

53. HYPOLIMNAS BOLINA.—Moore also gives *jacintha*, which is only a variety. Found also in Southern Asia and Australia, in Madagascar and in most of the tropical Islands in the Pacific.

In his key to the genus *Hypolimnas*, Bingham says *bolina* can be distinguished in India by having "fore and hind wings with a post-discal series of white spots always present." Specimens can be found in Ceylon with no trace of these spots on the fore wing, and only very minute specks on the hind wing.

Common at Haldummulla all the year round, but specially in December, when it appears in swarms in the tea. By walking it up in the evening, after it has gone to roost, it can easily be captured in any number, and a fine series of varieties selected. As is usual in Ceylon, both dry and wet season forms fly together.

The male is an exceptionally long-lived fly. A battered specimen will take up its position on one branch for several weeks, flying off to attack any fair-sized butterfly that passes. I have known them drive away *Kallimas* that wished to settle on sugar. They do not seem to be attacked at all by birds, or to take the slightest notice of them.

Localities: Everywhere from sea level to Nuwara Eliya.

54. HYPOLIMNAS MISIPPUS, De N., B., and E.; *Apatura misippus*, M.—Found in Asia, Africa, Australia, and North America.

Usually rather rare at Haldummulla, except at one spot in the tea here, where there is frequently a single male. In December, however, it often appears in great numbers. In these swarms the females are much commoner than the males, which is unusual at other times. The *chrysippus* form *(diocippus)* is always much commoner than the *dorippus* one, (*inaria*) though the latter is often plentiful. On one occasion I was walking to Tanamalwila, on the Wellawaya-Hambantota road, and *misippus* was in thousands, both males and females, settling on the road from about the 36th to the 28th mile. I could have caught any number of the *dorippus* variety, but could not find one perfect specimen. In the north, where the *chrysippus* form is abundant, I have only twice seen the *dorippus* form.

The *alcippus* form (*alcippoides*) with white lower wings is not I believe found in Ceylon, but I caught a specimen at Jaffna, which was very near it, having a small, but conspicuous, white patch on the upper side of the lower wing.

It seems to prefer the drier portions of the Island, but a few may be taken in the wet zone.

55. PYRAMEIS CARDUI, M. and De N.; *Vanessa cardui*, B. and E.

Commonly known in England as the Painted Lady. It is found all over the world "except in the Arctic regions and in South America" (De N.). It has since been taken within the Arctic circle in North Lapland.

Single specimens may be seen anywhere, all the year round, but in some localities great numbers suddenly appear, though it does not seem to flight I have noticed these big hatches at Galle (twice) and at Jaffna. I have also found the larvæ in great abundance at Galaha, near Kandy.

56. PYRAMEIS INDICA NUBICOLA. *Vanessa indica nubicola*, E.; *Pyrameis indica*, M., De N.; *Vanessa indica*, B.

Found in S. Europe, the Canaries, India, China, Japan, etc. The race *nubicola* is restricted to S. India and Ceylon, it differs in having the outer margin of the hind wing comparatively much more broadly black.

I have never caught it below 4,500 feet, but it is very common at times above that elevation. It is not difficult to catch, but the easiest way to get perfect specimens is to collect the pupæ. The larvæ feed on *Heterophylla palmata*, and tie the leaves into a ball about the size of an orange; the pupæ can be found inside these balls, which are very conspicuous. The best implements for collecting them are a pair of scissors and a biscuit tin, as the sting of the nettle is painful, though it passes off quickly.

The English stinging nettle has now appeared on the Golf Links at Nuwara Eliya and the larvæ can generally be found on it.

Localities: Nuwara Eliya, Haputale, Pattipola, etc., wherever the food plant grows.

57. VANESSA HARONICA, M. and De N.; *Vanessa canace haronica*, B.; *Vanessa (Kaniska) canace haronica*, E. Peculiar to Ceylon, and seems to deserve specific rank.

It differs from *canace* as follows: "The broad blue band is discal, not post-discal, and anteriorly is continuous with the broad short oblique bar beyond the cell, not commencing, as in *canace*, below the pre-apical white spot. On the hind wing the band is without the series of black spots, but beyond it there is a transverse post-discal row of small blue spots" (Bingham).

Specimens showing any signs of grading into *canace* are very rare. There is one specimen in the Museum collection in which the blue band on the upper wing is distinctly forked, the outer branch continuing to the pre-apical white spot. In a few cases, where the blue band is especially wide, there are distinct signs of the post-discal black spots on the lower wing. In general appearance, however, the two butterflies are very distinct. Moreover, according to authorities quoted by Bingham, their larvæ are most distinct, as follows:—

Canace.—" Segments alternately orange and white, with numerous black spots on the orange segments, and black streaks on the white. Seven white branching black-tipped spines on each orange segment."

Haronica.—"Light red, spotted with black, the segments divided by blackish and purplish lines, anal segment slightly humped, segments armed with eight longitudinal rows of yellow branched spines."

Common at Haldummulla and fairly easy to catch. It comes readily to sugar, but is very shy. Very common at Haputale and Ohiya, but seems scarcer at lower elevations, though a few have been taken at Galle.

58. KALLIMA HORSFIELDI PHILARCHUS, E.; *Kallima philarchus*, M, and De. N.; *Kallima horsfieldi*, B.

Peculiar to Ceylon, but it is questionable whether it is distinct from *horsfieldi*. *K. mackwoodi* appears to be the dry season form, in which the ground colour and discal band are paler in colour. The two discal hyaline spots are very variable in size in both the wet and dry season forms.

Rare at Haldummulla except in December. The flight nearly always starts in Christmas week and only lasts a few days. In December, 1914, they arrived early in December, and were plentiful for the whole of that month, but at a higher elevation they remained in fair numbers till April. During these flights they are common on the Horton Plains (over 7,000 feet) but seldom seem to reach Nuwara Eliya. In parts of the low-country of Uva they are often very abundant in July, but very few migrate up-country then. It is in this brood that dry season forms are most likely to be taken. They are extremely easy to catch, as they cannot refuse toddy, treacle, etc., especially if mixed with rum.

They are pursued by Drongoes (*Dicrurus leucopygialis*) but I have never seen one eaten, the bird almost invariably taking a triangular piece out of one of the lower wings. Whether he finds this distasteful or not I cannot say, but he never seems to continue the pursuit of that individual, though the next one to pass is probably treated in the same manner. At least 50 per cent. of those taken at sugar in open country will be found to have been damaged. The birds seem quite unable to see them when settled, though they do not make the most of their resemblance to a dead leaf. If settled on a twig with the tail towards the base, and the fore-wing well drawn out, the resemblance is perfect; but they usually settle with their heads towards the base, and the fore-wing more than half covered by the lower, when the resemblance is far inferior. When settled on tree trunks feeding on "sugar" they are very conspicuous to the human eye.

59. DOLESCHALLIA BISALTIDE, M. *Doleschàllia polibete*, De N.; *Doleschallia bisaltide malabarica*, B.; *Doleschallia bisaltide ceylonica*, E.

Bingham and Fruhstorfer agree in giving the Indian and Ceylon race as *malabarica*, but Evans writes, in his list: "There is not sufficient material in the British Museum to judge whether these races are worth retaining."

It is usually very rare at Haldummulla, but it sometimes appears in fair numbers in the tea in November and December. It settles, usually low down, on the side of a tea bush, so only gives room for a very awkward stroke with the net between the bushes; it also requires very careful stalking, so is seldom caught. I have not yet succeeded in attracting it with sugar or other baits.

60. ARGYNNIS HYPERBIUS TAPROBANA, E. *Argynnis hyperbius*, B.; *Acidalia niphe*, M. and De N.

A. hyperbius is found in India, Burmah, Abyssinia, China, Japan, etc., but apparently our Ceylon specimens form a local race, though they only differ in the slightly darker ground colour. They vary extremely little.

It is common at high elevations nearly all the year round, and is usually found on the patanas near jungle. It settles on the ground, or low down, and is very easy to catch as it only flies a short distance if disturbed.

I have seen two stragglers (♀) as low as Haldummulla (3,000 feet), but it is very rare below 4,500 feet.

Localities: Nuwara Eliya, Horton Plains, Haputale, Maskeliya; in fact, wherever the wild violet grows.

61. ATELLA PHALANTA, M. De N. and E. *Atella phalantha*, B. Found in Africa, India, Burmah, Malaya, China, etc.

Common at Haldummulla nearly all the year round, except in September and October, viz., the end of the dry season. Sometimes it flights in very great numbers. When flighting, it goes fairly fast and straight, but at other times it settles on flowers, etc., and is very easy to catch. In the dry low-country it swarms on wet patches on the roads.

Common from Galle to Jaffna and at all elevations up to 6,000 feet at least.

62. ATELLA CEYLONICA, Manders. *Atella alcippe ceylonica*, B. and E.

Peculiar to Ceylon. Differs from *alcippe* "in the broad immaculate black apex of the fore wing in both sexes and on the greater breadth of the terminal band on both fore and hind wings" (Bingham).

It is constant and well separated geographically, and I think deserves specific rank. *See* Plate I, fig. 2.

I know nothing of this, so asked Mr. Mackwood for particulars. He writes: "*Atella ceylonica* is a distinct species or sub-species. Major Manders described it. So far it has only appeared in one valley in the Nitre Cave, surrounded by 6,000 feet hills, except towards the north-west and east, where it faces the Bintenna country. The butterflies are found from 2,000 to 4,000 feet. Principal appearance, May-June. A few at end of the year."

I owe my specimens to Mr. Mackwood's generosity. He tells me that it was fairly plentiful at Nitre Cave in May and June, 1918.

63. ERGOLIS TAPROBANA, M., De N. *Ergolis merione taprobana*, B., E.

E. taprobana is also found in S. India; *merione* is found in India, Burma and Malaya. De Nicéville writes: "This species may be distinguished from *E. merione* by its darker colour on the upper side, the outer margin of the fore wing less falcate; it has also no sub-apical spot on the upper side of the fore wing of the male. On the under side of the hind wing in the male there is a large discal round suffused patch of dark maroon scales not mentioned by Mr. Moore,"

It is a well defined form which, in Ceylon at any rate, shows very little variation.

The wings, especially of the females, seem to split extremely easily, and perfect specimens are not too easy to procure. It is found at Haldummulla all the year round, but is only numerous during the flights. I have seen it at Galle, Jaffna, Mannar, etc., and up to 6,000 feet elevation at Ohiya.

64. ERGOLIS ARIADNE MINORATA. *Ergolis minorata*, M.; *Ergolis ariadne*, De N., B., E.; *E. ariadne* is also found in India, Burma, Malaya, Formosa, etc.

Moore has separated *minorata* as the Ceylon form, it differs in its smaller size.

It flights with the last (*E. taprobana*) at Haldummulla, but is more numerous, and is far easier to catch in perfect condition. It is found all over the Island, nearly all the year round.

65. BYBLIA ILITHYIA, M., De N. and B. *Byblia ilithia*, E. Also found in India, Africa, Arabia, etc.

It is apparently confined to the driest districts of the Island, and is extremely local and gregarious. In March, 1909, I found numbers settled on a small bush at Palatupane, in the Hambantota district, but have never met it there since. It is common at Giants Tank near Mannar, and I have specimens from Anuradhapura. If disturbed it flies off fast and low, but is almost certain to return in a few minutes, and it can be found in the same place day after day.

Acræinæ

66. ACRÆA (TELCHINIA) VIOLÆ. Also found in India.

It is very common everywhere from sea level to 6,000 feet at least, and occurs all the year round. The larvæ are very easy to find on *Cucurbitaceæ*, especially cultivated species, of which they are minor pests.

It can be found in the same place day after day, and is very easy to capture.

RIODINIDÆ

Libytheinae

67. LIBYTHEA MYRRHA RAMA, E. *Libythea rama*, M.

L. myrrha is found in India, Burma, Malaya, and China. *L. rama* is a race from Southern India and Ceylon.

Fruhstorfer separates the S. Indian race as *carma*.

Bingham says: "Var. *rama* (Moore) is the smallest southern and Ceylon form, with the orange markings much narrower and restricted, and the pre-apical double spots entirely white or white slightly suffused with yellow."

My specimens of *rama* also differ from *myrrha* in the shape and colour of the lower wings, which are more scalloped along the termen, and on the under side variegated with light and dark gray; while in *myrrha* they are uniformly coloured, without conspicuous markings.

Both forms fly together at Haldummulla and show very slight signs of grading, but in a large number of specimens which I have examined *the "rama" are always males and the "myrrha" always females*. This points to the conclusion that they are the same insect, and that *rama* is a race in which the male has varied from the original stock far more than the female. This point can, of course, be settled at once by breeding. The sexes can be easily distinguished by the fact that the fore legs of the ♂ are short hairy brushes, while those of the ♀ are functionally perfect.

They are almost always found settled on wet roads. If disturbed, they usually only fly a few yards, but if frequently put up, they may fly a little way off the road and settle on the bushes or grass; but in fine weather they will probably return to the road in a few minutes.

Both forms are plentiful at Haldummulla, but probably ten *rama* will be seen for one *myrrha*.

They are found from 500 to 5,000 feet in Uva, but so far I have not taken them out of the Province.

68. LIBYTHEA LEPITA LEPITOIDES. *Libythea celtis lepitoides*, B. and E.

L. celtis is found is Europe, Asia Minor, and Chitral; *lepita* is found in Assam and the Himalayas; and *lepitoides* is peculiar to S. India and Ceylon. *L. lepita* and *lepitoides* differ from *celtis* in the different shape of the hind wing, different shape of the orange band on the fore wing, and the absence of an orange spot in interspace 1. *L. lepitoides* differs from *lepita* in having the orange band divided, and all the sub-apical spots white, or nearly so. *See* Plate I., fig. 3.

It is extremely rare, and I have personally only caught a single specimen at Haldummulla. I have notes of its occurrence at Badulla and Wellawaya, and have received specimens from Kandy district.

Nemeobiinæ

69. ABISARA ECHERIUS, var. PRUNOSA, De N. *Abisara prunosa*, M.; *Abisara echerius*, B.; *Abisara echerius prunosa*, E.

De Nicéville says: *A. prunosa* is typically the darkest coloured, and, in the male, the most brilliantly purple shot of the group. It is mainly confined to S. India and Ceylon. The colour of the male is very difficult to preserve. It fades quickly and is usually badly damaged in the net, in fact it can only be seen well in freshly bred specimens. It is therefore an unsatisfactory feature on which to found a race. The markings, especially the black spots on the lower wing, show considerable seasonal variation.

It is almost always found in jungle. During the daytime it usually settles on a leaf five or six feet from the ground. If disturbed it flies a yard or two, and settles again. In the evenings, however, its flight conpletely changes, and it darts up and down a jungle path with a quick jerky flight, so that I have more than once mistaken it for one of the *Hesperiidæ*.

It is most plentiful at Haldummulla during the dry weather in the SW. monsoon. I have taken it at Kandy, Jaffna, Trincomalie, Galle, Ratnapura, and up to 5,000 feet at Haputale.

LYCÆNIDÆ.

Lycæninæ.

70. NEOPITHECOPS ZALMORA, De N., B. and E. *Pithecopos dharma*, M. Found in Southern Asia.

One of the most variable insects in Ceylon. The amount of white on the upper side varies as much in location as in amount. The principal varieties in my series are:—

(1) Upper side: both wings black, minute white speck or pale patch on disc of fore wing = *zalmora*.

(2) Discal white spot on fore wing much larger. Lower wing with a large white patch from the cell to the margin, between veins 4 and 7 = *dharma*, as illustrated in Moore.

(3) Fore wing about half white. Lower wing with five very minute sub-marginal white spots. The markings on the under side almost obsolete, except the black sub-costal spot on hind wing. (Only taken at over 5,000 feet elevation.)

Very common at times at Haldummulla, and apparently flights. A great number appeared in August, 1915, all flying west. They settle frequently, and usually close to the ground, and are easy to catch. Their wings, however, are very frequently rubbed in the net.

I have taken it from 500 to over 5,000 feet elevation in Uva. Also at Galle, Ratnapura, Trincomalie, Vavuniya, etc.

71. SPALGIS EPIUS. Also found in India, Burma, Java, Borneo, etc.

The male can be distinguished by its very sharp-pointed fore wings.

The larva feeds on coccidæ (scale insects), especially "mealy bug," and is never known to eat vegetable food. It does not resemble Moore's figure.

May be taken at Haldummulla all the year round, but is never numerous. I have also taken it at Galle, Kegalle, and Kandy.

71*a*. SPALGIS EPIUS NUBILUS, B. and E. Bingham gives this race also from Ceylon, and says two typical specimens in the British Museum are labelled "Trincomalie, Ceylon." Evans restricts it to the Andamans and Northern India.

It differs from *epius* as follows: Much darker ground colour, no white spot on fore wing of ♂, and only a slight pale patch on ♀.

S. epius varies considerably in the size of the white patch, especially the female, but I have not yet come across a specimen which quite answers the description of *nubilus*. The nearest approaches to it I have seen were a few dwarf specimens which had bred on "mealy bug" on some pot palms in the verandah of the Galle Hotel. Should it occur in Ceylon, I expect it would prove to be only a seasonal form of *epius*.

72. MEGISBA MALAYA THWAITESI *Megisba malaya*, De N., B., E.; *Megisba thwaitesi*, M.

In India there are two forms of *malaya*, one tailed, the other tailless. McDoherty states that "all my Kaumaon specimens, as well as those taken by me in Burma and Chittagong, are tailed, while in Orissa, Ceylon and the Eastern and Western Ghats, their place appears to be taken by a tailless form Of this last, those from Ceylon and the Western Ghats are apparently *Megisba thwaitesi*, Moore, but those from Orissa and the Eastern Ghats seem to me identical with *P. malaya*, except in absence of the tail." De Nicéville says: "I possess both forms from one locality only, i e., Sikkim." The few tailed specimens from Sikkim that I have seen were larger and more heavily marked on the under side than our forms, and I think the latter might stand as *Megisba malaya thwaitesi*, till breeding experiments have proved them to be only a variety of *malaya*, or a distinct species.

The male is very abundant in the low-country of Uva, and may be seen settled in dozens on the sand in river-beds, or on wet patches in the roads. The female, which has more rounded wings, is much scarcer

It is not rare at Haldummulla, but I have not seen it above 4,000 feet elevation. Other localities noted are Galle Kegalle, Kandy, Jaffna, Trincomalie, etc.

73. CHILADES LAIUS, De N., B. and E. *Chilades varunana*, M.

It is found in India, China, and Formosa, but not in Burma and Malaya.

C. varunana is the wet season form. The dry season form has a clouded brown patch on the under side of the hind wing. Both forms are very common all over Ceylon and fly together but the dry season one is the scarcer. They grade perfectly into one another. The female of both forms varies considerably in the amount of blue.

It may be taken at Haldummulla all the year round, but is only abundant during the NE. monsoon flights, when it is often the commonest blue for a few weeks. It is plentiful at Nuwara Eliya at times.

It is sometimes a pest of orange trees in India, as the larvæ feed on the young shoots.

74. CHILADES TROCHILUS, var. PUTLI. *Chilades trochilus putli*, E.; *Chilades putli*, M.; *Chilades trochilus*, De N. and B.

Fruhstorfer says that the genitalia prove this to belong to the genus *Lycæna*, not *Chilades*.

De Nicéville says: "The only difference between typical *C. trochilus* and *C. putli* is that the former has the orange markings above the marginal black spots on the upper side of the hind wing very prominent; while in the latter this colour is absent altogether, or replaced by ochreous." Bingham says: "var. *putli* is only the small Indian form which is identical with *trochilus* in ground colour and markings." *C. trochilus* is found in Europe, Asia, Africa and Australia.

It is so small that it may be easily overlooked, though it is generally found fluttering over the shortest grass, or nearly bare ground. It is essentially a low-country insect, but I took two specimens in 1916 on this estate (3,000 feet). These are both above the average in size.

Localities: The lawn in front of the Colombo Museum, Jaffna (very abundant), Mannar, Hambantota, Wellawaya, etc.

75. LYCÆNOPSIS AKASA. *Cyaniris akasa*, M., De N., B., E. Also found in S. India, Java, Sumatra, etc.

Moore describes the female as blue glossed, but not the male. Bingham says the female usually has no blue, but occasionally there are a few blue scales. I have never seen a female from Ceylon which showed any trace of blue. Bingham's figure is not at all like our Ceylon specimens; in neither male nor female is the black border of the fore wing extended to the tornus.

A very local insect but plentiful where it occurs. It is usually found near streams in the Hills, the male settling on wet patches on the roads, and the females hovering among the bushes, and settling frequently on flowers. It is common at Haldummulla and Haputale, especially during the NE. monsoon, March and April being the best months. I have also taken it at Nuwara Eliya.

76. LYCÆNOPSIS PUSPA. *Cyaniris puspa*, B. and E.; *Cyaniris lavendularis*, M. Found also in India and Malaya.

"Var. *lavendularis*, Moore, has the costal and terminal margins of both fore and hind wings more narrowly bordered with black than in typical *puspa*, but seems otherwise indistinguishable" (Bingham).

This seems a very constant feature of the males in Ceylon, and it is questionable if Moore's name should not stand for our race. I can see no difference in the genitalia of Ceylon and Indian specimens.

The males vary a great deal in the shade of blue, the amount of white, especially on the lower wing, and the clearness of the black marginal spots on the lower wing. Bingham says of these spots in *puspa* that "these are formed, not by actual scaling, but by the dark markings of the under side, which show through more or less clearly." This is not the case with Ceylon specimens, as the spots on the upper side are frequently far larger than those on the under side, and are occasionally very large and distinct above, when almost obsolete below. The female varies chiefly in the markings on the under side; in some specimens these are comparatively small and indistinct, especially on the hind wing.

The male is often very plentiful in the low-country of Uva,

settled in river-beds and on wet roads. It occasionally can be taken at Haldummulla. The female is very common at Haldummulla at times, and is apparently given to flighting. I have taken it here in every month but February and March.

The female bears no resemblance at all to the figure given in Moore.

77. LYCÆNOPSIS SINGALENSIS. *Cyaniris singalensis*, M. and E.; *Cyaniris huegeli singalensis*, B. Found in Ceylon, Java, and Sumatra.

Originally described from specimens taken at "Kalupahana, about 3,000 feet." I have no doubt this estate is referred to.

The male is very plentiful at high elevations. It is chiefly found settling in stream-beds or on wet roads. Occasionally I have taken specimens at Haldummulla, but they do not seem to descend below 3,000 feet. The female I have found extremely rare, and I know nothing of its habits.

78. LYCÆNOPSIS LANKA. *Cyaniris lanka*, M., B., E. Peculiar to Ceylon.

The male is extremely plentiful at high elevations. At Ohiya, Pattipola, etc., it is usually the commonest blue. It sometimes descends as low as 3,000 feet. It is nearly always found settled on damp spots on the roads. The female may be seen flying among the bushes, and settling occasionally at flowers. I have never taken one lower than 5,500 feet, but a native collector brought me several from Haputale (4,800 ft.).

"The larva feeds on *Smithia blanda*, which grows in the damper portions of patanas. The egg is deposited on the stem at the foot of the flower bud" (F. M. Mackwood in "Spolia Zeylanica," Vol. IX., Part XXXVI.).

79. LYCÆNOPSIS LIMBATA. *Cyaniris limbata*, B. and E.; *Cyaniris limbatus*, De N.

Also found in India and Sumatra. It is not mentioned by Moore. The male "differs from *C. singalensis*, Felder, only in the colour of the upper side being of a deeper shade; the markings of the under side in that species are perhaps placed rather more in echelon." (De N.). It differs from *C. lanka* in being rather lighter in colour on the upper side, and, on the under side in having the marginal spots enclosed in a lunular grey line which is absent in *lanka*.

I have taken the males at Haldummulla only, where it is not rare. They may be found settled on the wet roads in April, May, September and October. The females are very rare and I have specimens from Haldummulla, Haputale and Ohiya.

80. ZIZERA LYSIMON, De N., B. and E. *Zizera karsandra*, M.

Also found in Europe, Africa, Southern Asia, and Australia.

"Var. *karsandra*, Moore, is a pale form of *lysimon*." (Bingham.) Possibly it might rank as a race in Ceylon.

The male very closely resembles *Z. otis* but can be distinguished by the presence of a black spot in the cell, on the under side of the fore wing. Specimens from Jaffna have the marginal bands and spots very clearly defined, and one specimen taken there, a female, measures 26 mm. in expanse. I have seen *Z. maha* included in some Ceylon lists, but this last specimen is the nearest approach I have seen to that species.

It is common nearly everywhere in short grass from sea level to 5,000 feet at least. It occurs all the year round at Haldummulla, but is commonest in August and September.

81. ZIZERA GAIKA, De N., B. and E. *Zizera pygmæa*, M.

Found also in Africa, Arabia, India, and Malaya

Very common at low elevations, but gets scarcer above 3,000 feet. It may be found all the year round at Haldummulla, but is commonest in August. Usually found flying over short grass.

The larva is said to feed on *Lantana* blossom in S. India.

Localities: The low-country from Galle to Jaffna, but commonest in the drier districts.

82. ZIZERA OTIS, De N. and B. *Zizera indica*, M.; *Zizera otis indica*, E.

Found also in India, Burma, Malaya, Hong Kong, and Philippines.

Bingham says *indica* differs from *otis* in the great size of the discal black spots on the under side of the fore wing.

These spots vary very much in size, shape, and position, and the two posterior ones are often obsolete.

Very common everywhere from Galle to Jaffna, and from sea level to the Horton Plains. I have taken it in every month at Haldummulla.

83. AZANUS UBALDUS. Found also in India and Arabia.

The only places where I have taken this are at Elephant Pass, in the Jaffna Peninsula, and Giants Tank, near Mannar, but I have seen a single specimen from Trincomalie It is fairly common at Elephant Pass in December, but is very likely to escape notice. It is very small, and settles usually at a height of over 10 feet from the ground, at the end of a twig or thorn. If disturbed, it flies round very fast but soon settles in a similar place, and is not hard to catch When settled it closely resembles a small specimen of the next species, *A. jesous,* but that seldom settles so high up. It may be taken in plenty at acacia blossom at Giants Tank in July.

84. AZANUS JESOUS, B. *Azanus crameri*, M.; *Azanus jesous gamra,* E. Found in Africa, Arabia, and India.

Very common in the dry low-country, and is an occasional visitor to Haldummulla. It flies low, and is fond of settling at the end of a twig or large thorn, whence it apparently can get a clear view round. It is seldom seen more than two or three feet from the ground. It is usually found along road-sides in open country or scrub, very seldom in jungle.

Localities: Jaffna, Mannar, Anuradhapura, Wellawaya, Hambantota, Trincomalie, etc.

85. LYCENESTHES LYCÆNINA.

Also found in India, Malaya, and the Dutch Indies.

Fruhstorfer says true *lycænina* is only found in Ceylon, the Indian forms being races.

The male is very common at Haldummulla, and is always found settled on wet roads, or in the beds of streams, especially from March to May. If disturbed it flies round rapidly, but soon settles, and will allow one to miss it several times with the net before clearing off. The female is rarer here, and may be found settled on the tea, or on flowers. I found it very plentiful on the tea at Kegalle, but I never saw a male settled on the wet roads there.

Other localities are Galle, Hambantota, Wellawaya, Kandy, etc.

86. TALICADA NYSEUS.

Also found in India and Burma.

The upper side varies very little, but the late Mr. John Pole had several specimens in which the red patch was replaced by buff. The under side varies, especially in the number of the black spots on the lower wing.

It is exceedingly common wherever its food plant (Bryophyllum) grows, and is very easy to breed. The larvæ feed inside the thick leaves, only coming out to pupate. The affected leaves show the presence of the larvæ very clearly. It flies slowly, and settles frequently. In the evenings it generally roosts on flower heads in groups of four or five, so the finest specimens, and unusual varieties, can then be selected, and caught in the killing bottle. It does not go to roost till rather late so there is not much time to take them before dark.

It is plentiful all the year round at Haldummulla, and I have taken it at Galle, Hambantota, Wellawaya, Kandy, etc.

87. EVERES PARRHASIUS, M. *Everes argiades parrhasius*, E.; *Everes argiades*, De N. and B.

E. argiades is found in Europe, Asia, Australia, and America and is said to have been taken near Dover. The limits of *parrhasius* do not seem to have been defined yet.

Mr Bethune-Baker, in his address to the Entomological Society of London as President, in January, 1914, pointed out that the difference in the scales of *argiades* and *parrhasius* proved them to be distinct species; and Dr. Chapman says their genitalia differ.

The male varies little except in size; the female varies greatly, the ground colour above being sometimes brown, without a sign of blue, and at others pale grayish blue with a brown border at the apex and termen of the fore wing and along the costa of the hind wing.

It is very abundant at Haldummulla all the year round, and is common all over the southern half of the Island, up to 6,000 feet at least. I have, so far, no records of its capture in the North.

NACADUBA. This is a very difficult genus to name. No writers agree as to the species to be found in the Indian region. The species mostly have a wide range throughout the Indo-Australian region, and vary considerably in different localities and seasons, and there is a strong generic likeness in them all. Some species seem to grade into others, and, the greater the number examined, the greater difficulty there is in separating them.

Fruhstorfer has lately published a revision of the genus (Deel II aflevering 2, Zoologische Medeedelingen, s'Rijks Mus. van Nat. Hist. te Leiden) founded on the differences in the genitalia, but he seems to have had very little Ceylon material at his disposal, and he only allows us five sub-species, viz., *N. pactolus ceylonica* (=*macropthalma*, M.), *N. nora noreia* with *f. ardates* (=*ardates,* M. tailless and tailed), *N berenice ceylonica* (=*atrata,* B.) *N. atrata gythion* (=*plumbeomicans,* De N.), and *N perusia prominens* (=*prominens*, M.). He does not mention the following as found in Ceylon, *N. pavana, N. viola,* and *N. dana,* and has probably never seen *N. noreia*, Feld.

The differences in the genitalia, in all except the *nora* group, are apparently so marked that there should be little difficulty in naming the males correctly, but it is not so easy to decide as to which is the corresponding female This can only be settled by breeding.

I annex a table mainly following those given by De Nicéville and Bingham.

A Underside fore wing ; basal area without white strigæ.

*a*1. White strigæ broad and diffuse = *pactolus*.

*b*1. White strigæ narrow and clearly defined = *pavana*.

B. Under side fore wing; white strigæ on basal area.

a2. Apex of fore wing very acute = *viola*.

b2. Apex of fore wing not very acute.

a3. Basal strigæ not extended below median vein; no tail.

a4. Under side hind wing; small black spot in tornal angle, and much larger one in interspace 2 = *noreia*.

b4. Under side hind wing; small black spot in tornal angle and a very slightly larger one in interspace 2 = *dana*.

b3. Basal strigæ extended below median vein

a5. Expanse under 25 mm. = *ardates* tailed and tailless.

b5. Expanse over 25 mm.; tailed.

a6. White strigæ on under side fore wing, wide and often diffuse. ♂ wings transparent, markings of under side visible above. ♀ patch on fore wing and majority of hind wing white in some lights = *atrata*, B.

b6. White strigæ on under side fore wing narrower but clearly defined and prominent. ♂ wings slightly transparent, ♀ patch on fore wing and majority of hind wing blue, never white = *prominens*, M.

c6. White strigæ on under side of fore wing still narrower, especially in the ♂. ♂ darker, wings quite opaque. ♀ patch on fore wing darker and smaller, iridescent blue patch on hind wing small or absent = *plumbeomicans*, De N.

The great objection to this table is that it largely depends on the old fallacy that the exception proves the rule. For instance—the *ardates* and *atrata* groups are separated by the distinction of size, all under 25 mm. being classed as the latter. Specimens of the *atrata* group (*b5.*) under 25 mm. are very common and I have two or three which only measure 18 mm. in expanse.

Again an important division depends on whether the basal pair of strigæ are continued below the median vein. I have a series of tailed *ardates*, otherwise quite normal, showing every graduation from the strigæ stopping at the median vein till they reach vein 1.

Judging from Fruhstorfer's revision my nomenclature of the *atrata* group (*b*5.) is quite correct as regards the females, but very wrong in the identification of the males. I refer to this later when dealing with the individual species.

88. NACADUBA PACTOLUS CEYLONICA, Fruh. *Nacaduba macropthalma*, M.

Fruhstorfer says that an examination of the genitalia proves that *macropthalma* of the Nicobars, and *pactolus* of the Moluccas are races of one species, and that *pactolus* is by two years the older name. He states that races of *pactolus* are found in India and Malaya, and from Ceylon to the Solomon Islands, Formosa, and Amboina. He divides the Indian races into *macropthalma* from the Nicobars, *andamanica* from the Andamans, *ceylonica* from Ceylon, a new sub-species, unnamed, from S. India, and *continentalis* from Sikkim, Bhutan, Assam, and Burma. I have two specimens of *macropthalma* ♂ from the Nicobars, and consider them quite a distinct race from ours. A specimen from the Andamans is very like ours. Fruhstorfer distinguishes our race by the grey. black colour of the under sides. In all my specimens it is rather pale brown; the grey black form may be seasonal.

Taking the average it is our largest *Nacaduba*, one of my males being 39 mm. in expanse. The female usually has the blue area very large, the veins are clearly marked and there is a disco-cellular streak on both wings.

I have found it very rare and local and after over 30 years collecting have only a poor series of 12 specimens, from Haldummulla, Wellawaya, Ratnapura, and Kandy.

89. NACADUBA PAVANA NABO. Fruh. N. *pavana*, B. Was originally described by Horsfield from Java. The type of *pavana* is in the British Museum, but, being 100 years old, is

naturally badly faded. Fruhstorfer states that races of it are found in India, Burma, Siam, Dutch Indies, Malaya, etc. He does not mention it from Ceylon, but describes the Indian race as *pavana nabo*. He notes two forms of the clasp, one with distal teeth only, and the other with teeth along the dorsal edge. He suggests that the latter is the dry season form, but says his evidence is insufficient to prove it. Most of the Ceylon specimens I have examined show these dorsal teeth very strongly developed, but in five specimens from Kottawa and Deniyaya, (wet zone) they are absent, so he is almost certainly right. The clasps of our Ceylon form differ considerably from those of *pavana*, and I think it should rank as a species, not as a race. I have found similar genitalia in a specimen from Assam. *See* Plate 7, figs 2. and 3.

The males in Ceylon are usually slightly smaller than *pactolus ceylonica* ♂, and average far larger than the specimens of *pavana* I have seen from the Andamans. The females are easily separated from those of *pactolus ceylonica;* they are much smaller, ranging from 22—30 mm., the veins are not clearly marked, and there is no disco-cellular streak The blue area is very variable in extent, and they bear a strong resemblance above to what I call *prominens* ♀.

It is much more plentiful than *pactolus*, especially in the wet zone. I have found it abundant near Galle, and have specimens from Haldummulla, Wellawaya, Ratnapura, Deniyaya, and Kandy.

I have seen two ♂♂ with a rudimentary pair of basal strigæ.

90. NACADUBA VIOLA.

Also found in India, Burma, Malaya, Australia, etc. Fruhstorfer does not give Ceylon as a locality. The male can be distinguished at once by the very pointed apex of the fore wing, and the straight terminal margin of both wings. It varies greatly in size. I do not know the female, There are two specimens in the British Museum, named *viola* ♀ by Moore. They do not show the pointed wings of the male, but agree with the figure in "Lepidoptera of Ceylon." It would be very difficult to distinguish them from the females of what I call *plumbeomicans*.

It is apparently rare everywhere. I have taken about half a dozen males settled on wet roads at Haldummulla, and have specimens from Galle and Deniyaya. The genitalia agree with Fruhstorfer's figure of those of *viola* from Sumatra.

91. NACADUBA DANA.

Also found in India, Burma, Dutch Indies, New Guinea, etc.

Fruhstorfer, in common with all other writers, does not give Ceylon as a locality. He names the Indian race *dana dana*, and our form is apparently identical, both externally and in the genitalia.

It can be at once recognised by the fact that it is the only Ceylon *Nacaduba* which does not possess the conspicuous large black spot in interspace 2 of the under side of the hind wing. There is only a minute spot, nearly equal in size to the one in the tornal angle.

I have taken more than a dozen males settled on wet roads, or in beds of streams, at Haldummulla, and in May, 1916, I found it very abundant at Wellawaya, and also took one at Tanamalwila, on the borders of the Southern and Uva Provinces. I have also got it from Ratnapura.

It is tailless, and may easily be mistaken for a tailless *ardates* when settled, but is of a distinctly lighter blue when flying.

The female is very rare, and I have only taken two specimens

92 NACADUBA ATRATA, M. *N. atrata gythion*. Fruh.

93. NACADUBA PROMINENS, M. *N. perusia prominens*. Fruh.

94. NACADUBA PLUMBEOMICANS, De N. *N. berenice ceylonica*. Fruh.

This group has always given a lot of trouble. The species have a very extended range, and are very variable in different localities, and from seasonal causes, and no writers agree in their nomenclature.

Fruhstorfer has done good service in pointing out that the only certain way to identify the males is by an examination of the genitalia, which differ widely in each species, but there remains the difficulty of allotting the right male to the right female, and this can only be settled, with certainty, by breeding. The only Ceylon record of this that I can find is in "Lepidoptera of Ceylon" where it is stated that *prominens* feeds on *Vateria indica.* Bell has bred two species of the group in India, but I have not yet seen his specimens.

Fruhstorfer says we have three species in Ceylon, and I find this is correct, though there may be a fourth, as I have found four distinct forms of genitalia. Pending further investigation I can only describe the forms I have so far examined.

Males. *a.* A small form, paler blue than the others, wings rounded and transparent, the white strigæ below showing through very clearly. The strigæ are wider than in any other Ceylon form and are often very diffuse. The genitalia (Plate 7, fig. 8), do not agree with any of Fruhstorfer's figures, but are nearest to those of *berenice isana.* It may prove to be a seasonal form of *berenice ceylonica.* I have called it *atrata* in my table.

b. A large form attaining up to 36 mm. in expanse, darker than *a.* Wings rather pointed and only slightly transparent. The white strigæ below narrower, but very much broken up and tangled on the hind wing.

It resembles Moore's type of *prominens* in the British Museum collection and the genitalia are those of *perusia*, (Plate 7, fig. 5), so it is clearly Fruhstorfer's *perusia prominens.*

c. Smaller and slightly darker blue. Wings rounder, lightly transparent. White strigæ below slightly narrower, but much more regular.

The genitalia are nearest to those of *berenice plumbeomicans*, but have the "abnormal wide band" Fruhstorfer mentions as characteristic of *berenice ceylonica.* (Plate 7, figs. 6 and 7). I have classed it as *prominens* in my table, but I am clearly wrong in this.

d. Small and much darker. Wings quite opaque. Strigæ below very narrow and clearly defined. I have always regarded this as *plumbeomicans*, but the genitalia are unmistakably those of *atrata gythion* (Plate 7, fig. 4). Moore describes ♂ *atrata* as smaller and darker than *prominens*, so I think this will have to stand as a race of *atrata* in future.

Of the four forms *d.* is extremely plentiful, *a.* and *c.* are common and *b* is by far the rarest.

Females. *a.* Very variable in size (from 18-30 mm); patch on fore wing and most of hind wing white, with a dusting of blue scales; when the white patch is smaller than usual, there are often two or three diffuse white discal spots on the brown border, parallel with the terminal margin. White strigæ on under side exceptionally wide and diffuse. Horsfield originally named *atrata* from a female from Java "transmitting a white patch on the disc," and therefore De Nicéville and Fruhstorfer agree in naming this form *atrata*. The under side closely resembles that of male *a.*, so I have named both *atrata*.

b. Larger, a large patch on fore wing and most of hind wing pale blue. Strigæ on under side not as wide as those of *a.* It agrees with Moore's figure of *prominens* ♀ in "Lepidoptera of Ceylon," though the blue is a little darker, never white, so I call it *prominens*.

c. Very like *b.* but smaller. The blue slightly darker and often smaller in extent. Strigæ on under side narrower and better defined. De Nicéville and Fruhstorfer call this *prominens*. The under side agrees with that of ♂ *c.*, so I have called it *prominens*, though almost certainly wrongly.

d. Smaller, the blue area on fore wing smaller and much darker. The blue on hind wing absent or small in extent. Strigæ below very narrow and well defined. De Nicéville calls this *plumbeomicans*, and Fruhstorfer agrees. Moore apparently calls it *atrata*, which he describes as of a "more intense and darker blue" than *prominens* ♂.

The under side agrees with that of ♂ *d.*, so I have called both *plumbeomicans*.

a., c., and *d.* are common; *b.* is scarce.

To sum up, I pair ♂♂ *a. b. c. d.* with ♀♀ *a. b. c. d.* in that order on account of the similarity of the markings of the under side.

I have also noted that ♂ *d.* flights with ♀ *d.* Fruhstorfer names ♂ *d.* and ♀ *a. atrata gythion ;* ♂ and ♀ *b. perusia prominens ;* and ♂ *c.* and ♀ *d, berenice ceylonica,* closely allied to *plumbeomicans* Moore names ♂ and ♀ *b., prominens* and ♂ and ♀ *d, atrata.* De Nicéville names ♂ and ♀ *d, plumbeomicans.* Therefore the only species on which we agree is *prominens.* Confusion may have arisen through the wrong identification of the ♂ of typical ♀ *atrata,* from Java ; Fruhstorfer says *atrata, berenice,* and *perusia* all occur in Java. Of course the fact that *atrata* ♀ in Java has a white patch on the fore wing does not necessarily imply that the females of races of *atrata* elsewhere should show that patch, in fact, considering the variability of the genus, I consider it most improbable.

95. NACADUBA NORA (tailed).

95*a*. NACADUBA ARDATES (tailless) *Nacaduba noreia,* E.

Evans writes : " I believe with various other writers that *nora* and *noreia* are separate species ; *nora,* the tailed form, is also yellow below." Bell also believes them to be distinct. He has bred both and says the larvæ are very similar.

Personally I am of opinion that the two forms are distinct but I agree with Bingham and De Nicéville in thinking that the tailless form does not answer at all to Felder's description of *noreia,* which I consider quite a distinct species. Apparently *nora* should stand for the tailed form and *ardates* for the tailless

It is hard to define any difference between them, but the post-discal pair of strigæ usually appear to be nearer the terminal margin in the tailless form, and sometimes even touch the sub-terminal markings. The bands enclosed by the strigæ also seem comparatively broader. I have never yet seen the variety of the female with the yellow under side without tails, and in both sexes the tailed form is the most variable in the ground colour of the under side.

In the *atrata* group we had four forms, very similar externally, and apparently grading into one another, but readily separable by the very distinct genitalia of the males. In this group we have three forms, easily separated by their external differences, but whose genitalia are very similar, and difficult to distinguish. Fruhstorfer says there are also two "colour forms" of *nora*, in Sumatra, whose genitalia are apparently identical. As in the *atrata* group, breeding seems to be the only solution.

Tailed and tailless forms fly together all the year round, but the males are most often seen when the roads are wet.

They both vary much in the markings on the under side, and specimens can be taken of both in which the basal strigæ fail to reach vein 1.

I have seen a few specimens in Galle, Colombo, Jaffna, Trincomalie, Anuradhapura, etc., but they seem commonest in the hills. Common at Ratnapura.

96. NACADUBA NOREIA.

For some years past this name has been given to the tailless form of *ardates*, but Bingham points out that this does not at all agree with Felder's description. It was originally described by him from a specimen taken at Nuwara Eliya on December 24th, 1864, and for the next fifty years it apparently escaped the notice of collectors. I have now managed to collect a good series.

The five main distinctions are :—1. The external margin is less convex, 2. The basal strigæ on the under side of the fore wing do not extend below the median vein, 3. The males are a much brighter purple than *ardates*, and, in certain lights, have a broad purple-brown border. 4. The females have a very bright blue patch on both wings, as bright on the lower wings as on the upper; this I have never seen in *ardates*. 5. In both sexes the cilia at the apex of the fore wing are pure white, and on the hind wing they are paler than those of *ardates*. The fore wings are distinctly pointed, though not so much as in *viola*. The marginal spots on the lower wing of the female are obsolete, except in interspace 2, as Felder says; and the under side agrees with his description in every particular. It seems to vary very little. Mr. Riley exhibited a specimen at a meeting of the Entomological Society on 3rd March, 1920, and the following is an extract from the proceedings :—" *Nacaduba noreia*, Felder (female). This insect, described by Felder in 1864, has never since been correctly determined. The name has usually been applied to the tailless form of *N. ardates*. The species here exhibited, however, seems without doubt to be the true *N. noreia*, Feld., with the description of which it very well agrees."

I have had four males and two females from Haldummulla (3,000 ft.), thirty-four males from Wellawaya (500 ft.), and two females from Kandy (2,000 ft.). It was originally described from Nuwara Eliya (6,000 ft.), so has apparently a fairly wide range, and it is strange it has escaped notice for so long.

Capt. N. D. Riley has sent me a sketch of the genitalia. They are closely related to those of *N. nora*, if not identical.

97. LAMPIDES BOCHUS, B. and E. *Jamides bochus*, M. and De N.

Also found in India, Burma, Malaya, etc.

Bingham, speaking of Indian specimens, says that the black border of the males, measured on the dorsum of the fore wing, takes up one-fourth of the wing. In my Ceylon specimens one-sixth is nearer the average. The female varies far more than the male in this respect.

It is exceedingly abundant all over the southern half of the Island, and flies at Haldummulla all the year round. It often flights in great numbers, and these flights are usually composed of dwarf specimens 22-25 mm. in expanse. I have taken it from sea level to over 6,000 feet elevation, but have no notes of its capture in the North of the Island. The males sometimes settle on wet roads. It can usually be seen in quantity where *Boga medelloa* is planted for green manure, as the larvæ feed in the seed pods.

98. LAMPIDES ELPIS. Also in India and Malaya.

Common at Haldummulla, especially in March, April, and May. At times it becomes a pest in cardamom clearings, feeding on the blossoms and young seeds.

The male varies little, and the female only in the width of the black border to the fore wing, and size.

It is not given to settling on wet roads, but is usually found on bushes at the edge of jungle.

I found it very common near Galle in February and March, but have never seen it in the North of the Island. It is very plentiful at Kandy and in nearly all fields of cardamoms.

99. LAMPIDES CORUSCANS.

Peculiar to Ceylon and very local. The extremely dentate sub-marginal line on the under side distinguishes it at once from all other Ceylon species of the genus. The male varies little, but the female varies in the amount of blue on the upper side.

It is not rare in the jungles below Haldummulla, and I have found it gregarious, several being usually found fluttering round one small tree or bush. Other localities are Watering Point, Galle, Kottawa, Deniyaya, Balangoda, and Ratnapura.

100. LAMPIDES LACTEATA, B. and E. *Lampides pseudelpis*, M. De N. Peculiar to Ceylon.

Bingham thought it might be "an occasional variation" of *L. elpis* but it flies all the year round with that species and never shows any sign of grading.

The differences from *elpis* are very marked. In the ♂ it is best distinguished by the absence of the sub-terminal row of black spots on the hind wing, and the much narrower terminal black border of the upper wing. In the ♀ the ground colour is much paler, and the basal half of the costa is blue, not black as in *elpis*; it is much more like the female *celeno* than *elpis*. In both sexes the large spot in interspace 2 of the under side of the hind wing is very different, being larger and roughly pentagonal, instead of round as in *elpis*. The genitalia of the males differ from those of *elpis* and *celeno*. It is not given to settling on wet roads.

Not common at Haldummulla, but may be taken in May, June, November, and December.

I have also taken it at Wellawaya and Monaragala, and have received specimens from Ratnapura, Kandy and Deniyaya.

101. LAMPIDES CELENO, B. and E. *Lampides aelianus*, M., De N. Also found in India, Malaya, China, etc.

The upper side varies very little. The under side varies in the ground colour and markings, but I cannot see that the variations depend on climate in Ceylon.

The male is often seen settled on wet roads, but both sexes are more frequently found on the bushes and grass by the roadside.

The male has the same habit as *H. bolina* ♂ of taking up a position for days, and attacking every butterfly of about its own size that passes

Exceedingly plentiful all the year round at Haldummulla, and I have taken it from Galle to Mannar, but it is commonest in the south. It is common in Nuwara Eliya.

102. LAMPIDES BŒTICUS. *Polyommatus bœticus*, M., B., De N., E.

Also found in Europe, Asia, Africa and Australia. It is said to have been taken in England, and is included in English lists as the " long tailed blue."

It varies greatly in size, dwarf forms being very common. The female varies in the amount and shade of blue on the upper side.

It is common everywhere, at all elevations.

"In Mauritius it does great damage to garden peas." (Trans. Ent. Socy., 1919, Page cxi.)

103. CATACHRYSOPS STRABO.

Also found in India, Malaya, Australia, etc.

In his key to the genus *Catachrysops*, De Nicéville distinguishes *C. strabo* and *C. lithargyria* from the rest by " both sexes with a distinct small dusky costal spot between the disco-cellular and discal bands on the under side of the fore wing ; eyes hairy." This dot is sometimes absent in Ceylon specimens of *strabo*, and I have a specimen of *cnejus* which shows it. The hairy eyes seem to be the most reliable test. The males vary little, and the females only in the amount of blue on the upper side.

It is not given to settling on wet roads. It is especially

plentiful in abandoned low-country paddy-fields and chenas.

I have specimens from all over the low-country from Galle to Jaffna, but it becomes rare above 3,000 feet.

104. CATACHRYSOPS LITHARGYRIA.

De Nicéville and Bingham consider this to be only a variety of *strabo*. The former writes: "The two always appear to occur together, and the female of the latter species (*lithargyria*) is even now undescribed." Bingham writes: "Nor has any corresponding difference been found among the females, while in the blue males the markings are precisely the same as those of typical males."

Among the original sketches for Moore's "Lepidoptera of Ceylon," now in the Colombo Museum, there is an excellent plate of the female *lithargyria*, but for some reason it was not published. I therefore give one in Plate I. Fig. 5. The male differs, not only in colour and size, but in the shape of the wings, and on the under side the markings are far broader, better defined, and of an entirely different colour, the general appearance being very dissimilar. The female is much larger than any specimens of *strabo* I have seen, and the blue on the upper side is paler. The markings on the under side agree with those of the male, but are lighter in colour and broader. It is apparently constant, and shows no signs of grading into *strabo*. The male may easily be mistaken for *L. celeno* on the wing as the colour is the same, though paler. The genitalia closely resemble those of *strabo*.

It is very rare. I have taken one male and three females in the tea on this estate, and one or two males at Wellawaya settled on carrion, or wet patches on the roads. Mr. F. A. Fairlie tells me that in March, 1898, he caught several perfect specimens of ♂ and ♀ at Bakers Farm, Nuwara Eliya (6,000 feet), which is certainly not a locality for *strabo*.

105. EUCHRYSOPS CNEJUS. *Catachrysops cnejus M.*—

Also found in India, Malaya, China and Australia.

The males can be readily distinguished from other Ceylon species of *Catachrysops* by having on the upper side of the hind wing two nearly equal sized black spots, one each in interspaces 1 and 2. The females have both these spots crowned with orange. It is very variable in size and in the ground colour of the under side, and in the amount of blue on the upper side of the female.

It is very plentiful in the Northern Province, but very local elsewhere. It is rare at Haldummulla, and I have taken one specimen at Galle. In S. India it is frequently a serious pest to the gram crops.

106. CATACHRYSOPS PANDAWA LANKA, E.

106A. CATACHRYSOPS CONTRACTA NILA, E.

There are two very distinct forms of *pandava* in Ceylon, which apparently do not fly together, and might be separated as different races, if not species :—

(1) The large form. Average about 30 mm.

The male is a bright lavender-blue, with the veins very clearly marked. The fore wing with a brown terminal border over 1 mm. wide. Hind wing with a sub-terminal series of black spots, edged outwardly by a white line, the one in interspace 2 being sometimes inwardly bordered by red. Under side hind wing: sub-basal row of *four* black spots edged with white.

(2) The small form. Average about 20 mm.

The male is a rather dull violet-blue (almost matching *E. parrhasius* ♂), the markings of the veins very indistinct. The brown marginal border on the fore wing is extremely narrow, and the sub-terminal spots and white line on the hind wing are wanting, except in interspaces 1 and 2. Under side hind wing : sub-basal row of *three* black spots, of which the lower is often very indistinct.

The two females are very similar, but the smaller race have the blue on the upper side much darker, and on the under side show only *three* sub-basal spots instead of *four* The eyes are smooth.

The large race is very common in the low-country of Uva, and is a very rare visitor to Haldummulla. I have not taken it above 3,000 feet.

The males settle in numbers on wet patches on the roads

or on the sand in river-beds, and have rather a quick flight if disturbed. They usually, however, settle again quickly. The females are much scarcer, and are most likely to be found on weeds in abandoned paddy-fields or chenas.

The small form is apparently confined to the dry zone, and is extremely common in the Northern Province. Its habits are those of a *Zizera*, both sexes fluttering about together over short grass, and frequently settling on flowers. I have never seen the male on wet patches on the roads. It is especially plentiful at Elephant Pass (Jaffna) in December and January,

The only place where I have found both forms is at Trincomalie. I found two or three specimens of the large form in the Resthouse compound, and a few of the small form in Fort Frederick.

The genitalia of the two forms are very similar and show an extraordinary resemblance to those of *Chilades laius*.

Lt.-Col. Evans agrees with me that they are distinct, and has now named them as given above. Capt. Riley also believes that they are distinct species.

Mr. Bethune Baker has published a monograph on the genus *Catachrysops* in the transactions of the Entomological Society of London for 1922. (Plàte 275.)

He is of opinion that *pandava* and *contracta* do not belong to *Catachrysops*, but does not say in which genus they should be placed. Judging from the genitalia I am inclined to place them in the genus *Chilades*.

107. TARUCUS THEOPHRASTUS.

Also in North Africa, Socotra, Arabia, India, etc.

There are two varieties of the under side. In the first, all the black markings are very slender, and the post-discal band on both wings is a practically continuous slender line. In the second the markings are much broader, and sometimes rusty brown in colour. The post-discal band on the fore wing consists of six well separated oblong spots; and on the hind wing of eight spots, of which the middle three or four are crescent shaped. I have taken both forms together, and they apparently grade into one another, and I regard them as only seasonal varieties.

It is a very local fly, and only found in the dry zone. It is very abundant at times on the bund of Tissamaharama tank, and on the sand dunes at Kirinda, in the Hambantota district. Also on the bund of Murunkan Tank, near Mannar. It is fairly common at Kankesanturai, on the North Coast, and at Fort Frederick, Trïncomalie. It flies slowly close to the ground and settles frequently on flowers, so is easy to catch.

108. SYNTARUCUS PLINIUS.

Also found in Africa, India, Burma, Malaya and Australia. It is very plentiful at Haldummulla, and I have taken it in every month but December. Its range extends from sea level to over 6,000 feet. I have taken it at Jaffna, Mannar, Vavuniya, and Hambantota, but not in the wet zone.

They are fond of flying round plants of *Indigofera anil*, which is apparently the chief food plant at Haldummulla, and the males frequently settle on wet roads.

109. CASTALIUS ROSIMON. Also in India, Burma, Malaya, etc.

Very plentiful all over the low-country of Ceylon, but becomes rarer above 3,000 feet. It is commonest at Haldummulla in the dry season, June-August.

I have noticed it all over the low-country, from Galle to Jaffna. It prefers open country, and especially roadsides; flies slowly, and is very easy to catch. It settles in numbers on wet patches on the roads.

It varies a great deal in the amount of black on the upper surface, but the variation does not seem to depend much on climate. Several of my lightest-marked specimens are from Galle (wet zone), and my two darkest are from Haldummulla (medium) and Jaffna (dry zone).

110. CASTALIUS ETHION. Also in India, Burma, Malaya, etc. Much more a jungle fly than the last and is fond of settling on a twig or leaf projecting over a jungle path.

Is found nearly all the year round at Haldummulla, but is usually commonest in April and May.

It is common in the south of the Island, especially in the wetter districts, and I have taken it up to 5,000 feet elevation at Haputale. I have so far not taken it north of Dambulla.

111. CASTALIUS DECIDEA Also in India and Burma.

Fruhstorfer names our form *C. caleta hamatus.*

Moore also gives *C. hamatus,* but Bingham says this is only the wet season form. They certainly grade into one another.

In Ceylon the variation seems to depend very little on rainfall. Some of mine, with an exceptionally narrow band (viz., *hamatus*), were taken here in the dry season, and some with the broadest band were taken from March to May, when there is a fair rainfall. Others are from Galle, which is in the wet zone.

It is a jungle fly, with habits like the last, except that it apparently flights at times.

It seldom settles on wet patches on the roads

I have only taken it in the southern half of the Island, and never at any great elevation. It is very plentiful at times at Galle, and I have also taken it at Kegalle and Peradeniya.

Arhopalinæ

112. HORSFIELDIA ANITA NARADOIDES, with ♀ *f.* DARANA. *Amblypodia darana* and *naradoides,* M.; *Amblypodia anita,* De N., E.

A anita is found in India, Burma, Borneo, and Siam.

Capt. N. D. Riley has published a revision of the genus in 'The Entomologist." He points out that the type of *Amblypodia* is *A. apidanus* so that name cannot stand for this genus.

De Nicéville writes: "I believe *A. darana* to be a dimorphic female form only of the widely distributed *A. anita,* Hewitson; which form may possibly be confined to S. India and Ceylon." Moore says *darana* is larger than *naradoides,* the male being darker blue, and the marginal band narrower; the anal lobe is red only in the middle, its margin and the tail being black. The female is uniformly coloured above. I have not yet acquired any specimens of males answering to this description. Moore says it is found at Kottawa I have only one male from there, but it exactly matches all my other specimens on the upper side, and I fancy the male *darana* is only a seasonal form I have specimens of the brown female from Tangalle and Kandy and another with only a trace of blue from Haldummulla. By far the largest female specimen I have seen has a large blue patch. Both forms apparently fly together. The colour of the under side is very variable in both sexes and does not seem to be dependent on climate.

The males are very abundant in parts of the low-country of Uva, especially at Wellawaya. They settle in crowds on wet patches on the roads, or on carrion, and are strongly attracted by human perspiration. The females, however, are very seldom seen.

113. IRAOTA TIMOLEON, De N. *Iraota maecenas*, M.; *Iraota timoleon nicevillei*, E.

De Nicéville says that he thinks: "that it will hereafter be found the *I. timoleon* is the rains form, and *I. maecenas* the dry season form of one species." Bethune-Baker (A revision of the *Amblypodia* group) agrees with this.

According to De Nicéville, the two forms differ as follows: ' Hind wing, under side, with a large silvery irregular band below the costa, at right angles to the body = *timoleon*. India, China."

" Hind wing, under side, with no large silvery band below the costa = *maecenas*. India, Ceylon, China."

Both forms are found in Ceylon. All my specimens, with one exception, are *timoleon*.

The colour of the upper side is very sensitive to the influence of a relaxing box. Usually it is seriously dulled, but in some cases it changes to a distinct green I have noticed this failing in most of our *Amblypodias*.

It is very rare. I have taken a single specimen (*f. timoleon*) at Haldummulla in June, which appeared to be freshly hatched. The rest of my specimens are from Colombo, which appears to be its headquarters. I know nothing of its habits from personal observation. The male has one tail, the female two.

114. SURENDRA QUERCETORUM, var. DISCALIS, De N. *Surendra discalis*, M.; *Surendra quercetorum discalis*, E.

Discalis is smaller than *quercetorum*, which is found in India, Burma, and the Dutch Indies. (See my remarks in the preface.)

Formerly common at Haldummulla, but *Acacia cæsia*, its food plant, is apparently being killed out by *Lantana* here. I have also taken it at Wellawaya, Matara, Kegalle, Madampe, Dambulla, etc It is plentiful at Kandy.

None of my specimens show any conspicuous variation, except in size. It generally settles on a bush at no great height, and if disturbed flies a short distance only, so is easy to catch. Usually there are several specimens together, so if one is caught, an examination of the bushes near will probably lead to the capture of others.

115. AMBLYPODIA CENTAURUS PIRAMA. *Arhopala centaurus pirama*, De N. and E.; *Nilasera pirama*, M.

A. centaurus is found in Burma and Malaya; the race *pirama* is confined to S. India and Ceylon. It differs in both sexes in the brilliant blue colour on the upper side.

Variation in colour in Ceylon seems to be confined to relaxed specimens. Unrelaxed specimens are usually much brighter, and it is therefore difficult to separate a race on account of the brilliancy of its colour.

It is occasionally seen settled on wet patches on the roads in the low-country of Uva, and I found it once in abundance at Obergoda, on the Muppane-Pottuvil road, in June, in the dry bed of a river. It only flew a short distance and settled on the bushes, so was easy to catch.

I have specimens caught at Kandy and Trincomalie in April.

116. AMBLYPODIA AMANTES, Riley. *Arhopala amantes*, De N. and E.; *Nilasera amantes*, M.

Also found in India, Burma, the Andamans, etc.

It can at once be distinguished from the last by having a distinct lobe in the anal angle of the hind wing.

I have not yet taken it in Uva, but found it common near

Galle, on nutmeg trees. If disturbed it almost always returns to the same tree at once, so is very easy to catch.

I have specimens from Colombo and Ratnapura.

117. AMBLYPODIA ORMISTONI. Riley. sp. nov.

This butterfly was described by Mr. Riley in "The Entomologist," Vol. LIII. May, 1920. Figures of ♂ and ♀ will be found on Plate 1, figs. 4 and 4*a*.

In April, 1917, I procured seven males and one female at Nakiadeniya, near Galle. The jungle where they were caught has now been felled and planted with rubber, but the butterfly should be found in the same district, or at Deniyaya.

118. AMBLYPODIA ABSEUS MACKWOODI, ssp. nov.

The race is peculiar to Ceylon, and the description by Capt. Riley will appear in "Spolia Zeylanica," Vol. XII., part 46. See Plate 1, figs. 6 and 6*a*

Typical *abseus* is found in South Burma and Malacca; *A. abseus indicus,* in Sikkim, Darjeeling, Burma, Siam, and Annam. Our form resembles typical *abseus* more than it does *abseus indicus,* which has much broader black borders to both wings.

I have never taken this personally, though, when fishing at Ambawella (6,000 ft.) a small *Amblypodia,* settled close to me, which was either this or a new species. It is not very rare in the Hills above Ratnapura, and has been taken in Colombo.

118*a*. AMBLYPODIA BAZALOIDES.

Two specimens in the Colombo Museum collection have been identified by Capt. Riley as belonging to this species. They are badly damaged and have no label of place or date of capture, so constitute very unsatisfactory evidence on which to add a new species to our lists.

CURETINÆ.

119. CURETIS PHÆDRUS. *Curetis thetis,* B., De N., E.; *Curetis thetys,* M.

Dr. Chapman has published a revision of this genus, based on the genitalia, in "Nov. Zool." 22, p. 80, 1915. He says: "So far as I know *phædrus* is the only *Curetis* occurring in Ceylon, but it is surely highly probable that *thetis* occurs there also. What any particular records mean is of course doubtful, so long as *phædrus* and *thetis* are more or less confounded. On the other hand the *thetis* of Moore's "Lepidoptera of Ceylon" is no doubt *phædrus*."

From the key he gives it appears that in *thetis* the harpe has a "lateral (or rather ventral) process." In *phædrus* the "harpe is simple." Can the variation be seasonal? I believe there is only one species in Ceylon.

Very common in the drier parts of the low-country. The male is very plentiful at Wellawaya, and is almost always found settled on wet roads and in river-beds. The female is scarce there. At Anuradhapura I have found the male scarce, but the female common. I have specimens from Elephant Pass (Jaffna), Mannar, Dambulla, etc., and have taken one on this estate (3,000 feet).

It is a most variable insect. I have a few males, which correspond exactly to Bingham's description of var. *arcuata*, and there is a similar one in the Colombo Museum. My other males vary much in the shape of the wings and in the width of the black border on the fore wing; this border is almost always produced a short way up each vein of both wings. All varieties fly together.

The female usually has far less white than in Bingham's description and plate. In only one of my specimens does it reach to vein 1. I have never seen the form with this patch yellow in Ceylon.

Theclinæ

120. ZESIUS CHRYSOMALLUS.

Also found in India.

A common low-country fly, but the male is not rare at Haldummulla, April to August.

I found it extremely abundant at Kegalle, both sexes being equally plentiful on the tea, October to February. It is not rare at Galle, Jaffna, Mannar, and Trincomalie.

The male varies very little, but the female is most variable in the quantity and colour of the blue on the upper side. In some of my specimens it is reduced to a few blue scales at the base of the fore wing, while in others the wings are pale or dark blue, with a brown border.

I have found the pupa on the stem of an *Albizzia moluccana*. The larvæ are always attended by the large red ant, and the perfect insect may be looked for wherever these ants' nests abound.

121. CAMENA DEVA, De N. and E. *Pratapa deva*, M.

Found in India, Burma, Java, Philippines, etc.

A very local insect. For many years past I have always been able to find the males basking on one tree (*Ficus arnothiana*) on this estate from April to November. This tree grows at the top of a jungle-clad precipice. The female is extremely rare and I have only taken four, all on the tea on this estate; it can be easily distinguished from the female of *Tajuria longinus* by the absence of the post-discal black band on the upper side of the hind wing.

I have never seen it in any other locality, nor have the native collectors ever brought me a specimen.

SPINDASIS. This genus has been previously known as *Aphnæus*. It is quite the most difficult genus to name, and I confess that I am quite unable to hazard a decision as to how many species should appear in a Ceylon list. Moore's "Lepidoptera of Ceylon" gives four species: *Schistacea, fusca, lazularia* (= *lohita*), and *ictis*. De Nicéville gives *schistacea, vulcanus, fusca, lohita, zebrinus, ictis*, and *nubilus*; but he thinks that *fusca* and *schistacea* are only "varietal forms" of *vulcanus*; that *zebrinus* is probably a variety of *lohita*; and that "*A. nubilus* is a varietal form only of *A. ictis*." He thus reduces our species to three only. Evans gives *schistacea, fusca, lohita, ictis*, and *lilacinus abnormis*. "Lepidoptera Indica" gives *schistacea, vulcanus, fusca, lohita, zoilus*, (= *zebrinus*), *greeni, minimus, ictis*, and *lunulifera*, (= *nubilus*).

Every species is variable, some greatly so, and freaks are not rare. Something might be done by breeding on a large scale, but the larvæ unfortunately require the attention of certain species of ants, so it is by no means a simple matter to breed them.

Capt. N. D. Riley is at present engaged on a revision of the genus, mainly by examination of the genitalia, but the difficulty of the work is delaying its publication.

122. SPINDASIS LOHITA, De N. and E. *Aphnæus lazularia*, M.

Also found in India, Malaya, China, etc.

Fruhstorfer says *lohita* is from Java; *himalayanus* from N. E. India, *concanus* from S. India, and *lazularia* from Ceylon. De Nicéville says he cannot find the slightest character by which *lazularia* can be distinguished from *lohita*. It is the largest Ceylon *Spindasis* and the easiest to distinguish. It varies comparatively little on the upper side but the colour of the under side varies greatly.

It is usually gregarious, and if one is found, a search near will probably put up others. It is very fond of the blossom of *Microglossa zeylanica*, in common with most other species of *Spindasis*.

It used to be common at Haldummulla, but I have seen only one specimen there for many years. In February, 1916 it was very plentiful at Watering Point, Galle, and I have taken it at Hambantota, and have specimens from Ratnapura.

Its flight is very rapid, but it usually only goes a short distance and is easy to catch.

122*a*. SPINDASIS ZEBRINUS.

Described by Moore from Ceylon. It is found in S. China.

It differs from *lohita* in having the bands on the under side black, or black tinged with red. De Nicéville said he had a single female specimen of *lohita* from Ceylon which showed this character; it was almost certainly only a variety of *lohita*. I have never seen a specimen.

123. SPINDASIS VULCANUS FUSCA, E. *Aphnæus fusca*, M.; *Aphnæus vulcanus*, var. *fusca*, De N.

Fruhstorfer gives *vulcanus* and *fusca* as distinct species from Ceylon.

De Nicéville distinguishes *vulcanus* from *fusca* as follows:— *A*. "Male, upper side, hind wing (normally) not glossed with blue = *vulcanus*. *B*. Male, upper side hind wing glossed with blue = *fusca*."

Evans says of Ceylon specimens: "The orange anal patch on hind wing below is not extended upwards along dorsal margin as in continental specimens." i.e., *vulcanus*. Our form rarely has the hind wing glossed with blue, and I have had specimens from Madras that seemed identical in all respects with specimens from Ceylon.

The commonest *Spindasis* in Ceylon. It varies greatly in the amount of orange on the fore wing, and in size. On the upper side of the hind wing the orange anal patch is sometimes continued nearly the entire length of the termen.

I have found it in the greatest abundance at Kankesanturai, on the north coast, in December and January. Very common at Elephant Pass and Giants Tank in the Northern Province, on the hill behind Haldummulla Post Office, at Hambantota, and Tangalla. I have also taken it at Haputale, Kandy, etc., but not, so far, at Galle.

Its habits are the same as the last, and it is even easier to catch. At Kankesanturai I used the killing bottle instead of the net, as they were so difficult to disturb when feeding at flowers.

123*a*. SPINDASIS MINIMA, M. *Spindasis fusca ab. minima*, Riley.

Peculiar to Ceylon, and named from a single specimen which is in the British Museum collection. The illustration in "Lepidoptera Indica" is exceptionally bad and the locality of capture is not given. The under side is very distinct from that of any other Ceylon *Spindasis* and it is the smallest form we have, measuring only $\frac{9}{10}$ in. in expanse. Capt. Riley has examined the genitalia, and found them closely allied to, but distinct from, those of *fusca*, and I understand that he decides that it is impossible to create a new species from a single specimen, in a genus where aberrations are as common as in *Spindasis*, and he classes it therefore as an aberration of *fusca*.

124. Spindasis schistacea.

Also found in India and Burma.

De Nicéville thinks it is only a variety of *fusca*. He says *fusca* has the red bands on the under side broad, and *schistacea* has them narrow in both sexes. The female of *schistacea* has the upper side of both wings "more or less sprinkled with plumbeous scales," which is never the case in the female of *fusca*.

I believe it to be quite distinct. The females differ usually, as De Nicéville states, though occasionally a slight plumbeous scaling is found on *fusca* ♀. The males are not always so easy to separate, but the blue gloss on the hind wing of *fusca* is small in extent, if present at all, and is of quite a different shade to that of *schistacea*. The width of the bands on the under side is very variable, and useless as a test. It is common on a patana ridge near Haldummulla resthouse, and at Haputale, and I have taken a few specimens at Kankesanturai, Elephant Pass, Trincomalie, Hambantota and Kurunegalle.

125. Spindasis ictis ceylonica.

Fruhstorfer gives *ictis* as confined to Ceylon, and *lunulifera* to Sikkim.

This is the most difficult group to name, and I can at present only treat it as a number of local forms. The principal ones are:—

No 1.—Very plentiful in the Northern Province.

♂.—Upper surface dark brown, with a variable, but usually well-defined, orange patch on fore wing; a patch of light blue iridescence along the dorsum: lower wing brilliant iridescent blue; anal patch usually pale red, with rather large diffuse black spots.

♀.—Ground colour slightly paler, orange patch much larger, occasionally occupying one-third of fore wing; dorsal portion of fore wing, and the whole of the hind wing, except anal patch, covered with pale gray-blue scales. In both sexes the marking of the under side appears on the orange patch with exceptional clearness.

Under side, both sexes: very pale gamboge-yellow with darker markings, occasionally varying into khaki or even very rarely pale reddish-brown. The markings are always very clearly defined. This is I believe typical *ictis ceylonica*.

I have caught and examined some hundreds of these at Jaffna and Mannar, and, except for three abnormal specimens, they seem a fairly constant race or species. One freak is a ♂, upper side both wings pale reddish-brown, with slight blue iridescence on lower wing. No sign of an orange patch on fore wing. Under side pale khaki-brown, the markings very indistinct, and broken up into more or less round spots with dark borders and silver centres. The other two are ♂ and ♀, only varying in entirely wanting the orange patch.

No. 2.—Somewhat resembles the last, but is larger and darker; the orange patch is very small and very indistinct; the under side is reddish-brown *with well-defined markings*. I have a single specimen of No. 1 that nearly matches it on the under side, though very distinct above. This was very plentiful in the Hambantota district in July, but I did not succeed in catching a ♀. I have taken two ♂♂ at Haldummulla.

Capt. Riley thinks this is the wet season form of *ictis*.

No. 3.—Very near No. 2 on the upper side, except that it is larger and the orange spot is sometimes absent.

The under side is reddish-brown. The markings are *very indistinct*, consisting of slender silver lines and a few black scales. Even the anal patch is merged into the rest of the ground colour, and the usual black spots are absent.

This is found on the Uva patanas at high elevations, and I have seen specimens from Badulla. Capt. Riley thinks it is the dry season form of *ictis*.

126. SPINDASIS LUNULIFERA FAIRLIEI.

This is found in the North of the Island. It is very like my race 3 of *ictis* and my meagre descriptions led Mr. Fairlie to confuse them. Capt. Riley writes: "The '*fairliei*,' so called by me, is smaller, has the bulk of the fore wing as well as the hind wing purplish suffused, an occasional bright orange but very small patch on fore wing, and the under side rather of the wet type." Mr. Fairlie, the original discoverer, writes: "At Manipai, Jaffna, I took races 2 and 3 of *A. ictis*, with race I. and I consider these to be quite distinct from *A. ictis* No. I. The blue iridescence on both wings of the male is more violet than in the *Aphnæus* you describe under *A. nubilus*, and spreads over a larger area of the fore wing in my specimens, and the under sides are paler red." See Plate 2, figs. I. and I*a*.

The genitalia prove it to be a race of *S. lunulifera*.

126*a*. SPINDASIS GREENI. *Spindasis lunulifera ab. greeni Riley*. Described from a single male captured at Pundaluoya. Evans thinks it a casual aberration of *S. fusca*.

The genitalia prove its connection with *S. lunulifera* though they differ slightly from those of that species.

As in the case of *S. minima* Capt. Riley does not see his way to create a new species in this genus from a single specimen.

127. SPINDASIS NUBILUS, M.

This is treated in "Lepidoptera Indica" as a variety of *S lunulifera*. The genitalia prove it to be allied to, but distinct from, that species. In Ceylon it is apparently confined to the Northern Province.

Male:—Upper side—ground colour dark black brown, a dark blue iridescence covering the lower half of the fore wing, and all the hind wing, except the anal patch which is dark red. The upper side resembles that of *A. lohita*, male, under side dark brick red with clearly defined markings; anal lobe with two large black spots, with a border above varying from orange to deep red.

Female:—Upper side—ground colour lighter than in the male; a small very diffuse orange spot on fore wing, the blue iridescence of the male being replaced by a dusting of grey blue scales. Under side as in the male.

The very deep red of the under side is in striking contrast to the gamboge yellow of *A ictis* No. I., with which it is found and they can at once be distinguished from one another, when settled, as far as they are visible

It is fairly common at Elephant Pass, Jaffna, and I have also taken it at Giants Tank, Mannar.

Mr. F A Fairlie writes: "Under *A nubilus* you describe a butterfly I have taken many specimens of at Iranaimadu Resthouse, about 50 miles from Jaffna on the North Road, which I think has not yet been named. I took it with an equal number of *A. ictis* race I., and it is certainly quite distinct."

I have sent four or five specimens to the British Museum.

127*a*. SPINDASIS LILACINUS ABNORMIS.

This name had been given to a pair of *Spindasis* in the Colombo Museum collection. See plate 2, figs. I. and I*a*. They were taken by the Museum collector at Illupakadavai about 20 miles north-east of Mannar.

As there was reason to doubt their being correctly named they were sent to Capt. Riley for examination. He says they are ♂ and ♀ of *S. lunulifera fairliei* (No. 126 above.)

128. TAJURIA LONGINUS.

Also found in India, Burma and Malaya. Fruhstorfer gives *longinus* as the Ceylon race of the Indian *cippus*.

The larvæ feed on *Loranthus*. Neglected orange and lime trees are always infested with this parasite, and a stone thrown into the tree will often put up a number of the butterflies; they fly round rapidly but soon settle again. It apparently hatches out in the early morning, and requires a few hours before it is able to fly fast. If these freshly hatched ones are disturbed they will fly slowly for a short distance and settle, and can easily be caught in splendid condition. It comes to flowers, especially *Pointsettia*.

It is very common at Haldummulla, and in the Northern Province.

129. TAJURIA ARIDA, Riley, sp. nov.

To be described by Capt. N. D. Riley in "Spolia Zeylanica," Vol. XII., part 46.

The only known specimens are 2 ♂♂ and 3 ♀♀ which I took at *Pointsettia* blossom in my garden in Sept. 1918, in company with numerous *T. longinus*. The drought for the previous four months had been exceptionally severe.

The male mainly differs from *longinus* ♂ in its "dull frosted greyish blue" colour, without any of the iridescence of *longinus*. The females are more difficult to distinguish, but the post-discal band on the upper side of the fore wing is composed of fine lines for the whole of its length, whereas in *longinus* ♀ the anterior portion widens out into oval black spots.

130 TAJURIA JEHANA CEYLONICA, ssp. nov.

A local race of *T. jehana*, first discovered by Mr. F. A. Fairlie, and described by Capt. Riley in "The Entomologist" for Sept. 1921 (Vol. LIV.). It differs from typical *jehana* in the greater extent of the blue area on the fore wing above. See Plate 2, figs. 2 and 2*a*.

It is apparently confined to the Northern Province, and the only place that I have seen it is between Kankesanturai and Kirimalei on the north coast in July, August, December, and January.

I found it plentiful on a hedge of *Todalia aculeata*, which was in blossom in December and January. I only captured a few, intending to take more later, but for the rest of my stay in the district the weather was so bad that I got no more.

It was in company with *T. longinus*, but was easily distinguished by the different gray of the under side, and smaller size.

In July, 1916, it was very plentiful in the same place, at tamarind blossom. The wind was, as usual at that time of year, very strong, and the butterflies kept to the sheltered side of the trees, and were easy to catch with a long-handled net.

131. CHLIARIA NILGIRICA, E. *Hypolycæna nilgirica*, De N., M.

Also found in S. India.

A very rare insect. The males may be taken settled on wet roads, or in beds of streams, at Wellawaya, and I have taken one female at Haldummulla. Mr. F. A. Fairlie took specimens at Jaffna and Mr. F. M. Mackwood gives Matale, Heneratgoda, Dolosbage and Puttalam, as localities.

132. CHERITRA FREJA JAFFRA, De N. and E *Cheritra pseudojaffra*, M.

The race *jaffra* is also found in S. India ; *freja* is found in N. India, Burma, Malaya, etc. Fruhstorfer says *pseudojaffra* is the S. Indian and Ceylon race of *freja*. It is smaller than *jaffra*.

De Nicéville writes: " Of the characters given as distinguishing this species, I find that the colouration of the under side is the only constant one, the rest being variable. This single character is very slight, and it would perhaps have been better to have treated *C. jaffra* as a local race only of *C. freja*. I do not understand how Mr. Moore could have described *C. pseudojaffra* as a distinct species. My Ceylon specimens are identical with S. Indian ones of *C. jaffra*." The illustrations of *jaffra* in "Lepidoptera Indica" match our specimens. Evans says the Ceylon race only differs from *jaffra* in size.

Not rare in the low-country of Uva, but has a habit of settling too high for an ordinary net to reach. Generally several will be found together.

I have taken it at Wellawaya, Telulla, Tanamalwila, Kumbukkan, and Hambegama, in the low-country of Uva, and have specimens from Ratnapura.

133. RATHINDA AMOR. Also found in India.

Found all over the Island, from sea level to 3,000 feet at least. Fairly common at Haldummulla. Plentiful at Galle and Jaffna.

Settles on bushes, and flies a very short distance if disturbed. I have seen the larva feeding on *Ixora* blossom at Galle, and the red protuberances exactly matched the unopened buds.

134. HORAGA ONYX CINGALENSIS, E *Horaga ciniata*, M.; *Horaga cingalensis*, De N.

Peculiar to Ceylon, but possibly only an insular race of the Indian *H. onyx*. It differs in the narrower white discal band on the under side of the hind wing, in having the upper tail much shorter, and in its brighter blue colour. Usually very rare and local. It was plentiful at Kandy in August, 1918, and I have seen specimens from Kottawa and Deniyaya. I have never, personally, caught a specimen.

135. CATAPÆCILMA ELEGANS.

Found in India, Burma, and Malaya.

Fruhstorfer gives *elegans* as from Borneo, with race *myosotina* from S. India and Ceylon.

When I first came to this estate in 1889, this butterfly was plentiful on one field of tea. An adjoining chena was then cleared, and it entirely disappeared, and I never saw another specimen till August, 1915, when I took a male near Haldummulla kaddies. I have since obtained two more specimens from Haldummulla.

I have never come across it in my travels, and the native collectors have never brought me a specimen, so it must be very rare, or local.

136. LOXURA ATYMNUS ARCUATA, E. *Loxura arcuata*, M.; *Loxura atymnus*, De N.

L. atymnus is found in India, Burma, Malaya, China, etc. *arcuata* is the common form in Ceylon. De Nicéville thinks it not even worthy to rank as a local race. Fruhstorfer thinks the opposite.

It varies greatly in the shade of the ground colour, the amount of black on the lower wing, and the markings on the under side I have noticed that the colour fades a great deal if it is left too long in the cyanide bottle.

It is very common in the southern part of the Island, and is generally seen fluttering along the edges of jungles or chenas.

137. DEUDORIX EPIJARBAS.

Also found in India, Malaya, China, etc.

Common at Haldummulla, especially when flighting. There was a very large flight in August, 1915, travelling west, and small ones often arrive about December.

I noticed an exceptionally large flight at Pattipola in November, 1917, flying south.

I have also taken it at Galle, Hambantota, Jaffna, Mannar, Anuradhapura, and Ratnapura.

The male varies in the amount of red, especially on the lower wing. This red changes to deep orange if left too long in the cyanide bottle. The female seems very constant.

Is fond of settling on the tea and on low bushes, but flies off very strongly if disturbed, and cannot be relied on to settle again quickly. It is a serious pest of pomegranates in India.

138. VIRACHOLA ISOCRATES, M., De N. and E. *Deudorix isocrates.*

Also found in India.

I found it in fair numbers on the blossom of *Derris scandens* at Murunkan, near Mannar, in July. I have also taken it at Elephant Pass, Jaffna, at Wellawaya, and at Kirinda, in the Hambantota district. The females are much rarer than the males.

The larvæ are at times a pest of the pomegranate in India, and have also been reported as feeding in the fruits of apples, plums, peaches, oranges, loquats and guavas. In Ceylon I fancy it mainly feeds on the woodapple, as I have always found it near those trees.

139. VIRACHOLA PERSE, M., De N. and E. *Deudorix perse*

Also found in India. Fruhstorfer has separated the race from S. India and Ceylon as *Deudorix perse ghela.* Ghela is the Indian name for the fruit of *Randia dumetorum,* which is a favourite food of the larvæ.

I have found it very rare. I got a few specimens in February at Kirinda in the Hambantota district, and have taken it at Wellawaya and Hambegama Tank, in the low-country of Uva.

140. RAPALA SCHISTACEA Found in India and Malaya. Not mentioned by Moore.

Usually very common at Haldummulla all the year round, I believe the larva feeds on tea blossom *inter alia.* It is always to be found on tea which has run some time from pruning; if disturbed it flies very rapidly round and settles quickly, generally on the same bush, so is easy to catch. It visits flowers freely, and seems especially fond of *Pointsettia.*

I have taken it at Anuradhapura, at the blossom of *Micasea scandens*, and also at Jaffna and Trincomalie.

141. Rapala lazulina, M *Rapala varuna*, E. *Rapala orseis*, De N.

Also found in India. De Nicéville thinks it is identical with *R. orseis* (=*varuna?*) of India, Burma, Malaya, etc. Fruhstorfer says *varuna* does not occur in India, but is Javan.

It can at once be distinguished from *R. schistacea* by the much broader bands on the under side. The male has none of the brilliant blue iridescence on the upper side of the hind wing that *schistacea* has.

It is rare at Haldummulla, but I have taken a few at *Duranta* blossom. It becomes commoner at lower elevations in Uva, and I have specimens from Kandy, Anuradhapura, Galle, and Ratnapura.

142. Rapala lankana, De N. and E. *Deudorix lankana*, M

Also found in S. India.

A great rarity, and apparently confined to the wet zone A native collector brought me a specimen, said to have been taken at Colombo. My other specimens are from Ratnapura and Deniyaya.

143. Rapala melampus.

The exact range of this species is uncertain, but it, or an allied form, is also found in India, Burma, Dutch Indies, etc. Fruhstorfer said *melampus* was confined to S. India and Ceylon, but later on modified his views and confined *melampus* to Mussoorie. It is doubtful if he ever saw a Ceylon specimen. There are none in the British Museum. Our form may prove to be a new sub-species.

Mr. F. A. Fairlie took it at tamarind blossom at Manipai, Jaffna, in July, and I took one male at the blossom of *Todalia aculeata* near Kankesanturai, on the north coast.

I have heard of no other captures.

The upper side of the ♂ is bright red, and of the ♀ dull brick red and they may be easily mistaken for *D. epijarbas*; in fact I mistook my only specimen for *epijarbas* when I first saw it in the net. See Plate 2, fig. 3.

144. BINDAHARA SUGRIVA, De N. *Bindahara phocides*, M. *Bindahara sugriva moorei*, E.

Fruhstorfer says, *B. phocides* is found from Sikkim to Burma, with race *moorei* from Ceylon. He confines *sugriva* to Java. De Nicéville writes: "The male of *B. sugriva* is easily enough recognised by the blue fascia on the upper side of the hind wing, but I can find no character by which to distinguish the female of this species from that of *B. phocides*."

The larva feeds inside the fruit of a creeper, called by the Singhalese *Himbatu* (*Salacea reticulata*). An examination of these fruits will often show the eggs, usually near the stalk, and a hole by which the larva has entered. Curiously enough there are almost invariably two or more eggs, but I have never found more than one larva in the fruit.

When fully fed it leaves the fruit, and evidently burrows into the bark of some tree. I had great difficulty in rearing them at first, as, if they could not burrow to pupate, they died. I then gave them a sheet of cabinet cork, and it seemed to be just what they wanted ; the burrows were usually about one inch long.

Note.—Do not cut open the fruit to get the larvæ, or they will probably die.

My specimens show very little variation, except in size.

Common at Haldummulla and I have also taken it at Galle, Kegalle, and Kandy, and found it plentiful at the hot springs near Trincomalie in October.

PAPILIONIDÆ.

Pierinæ.

145. NYCHITONA XIPHIA, M. *Leptosia xiphia*, B., E. Also found in India and Malaya.

Very common in jungles all over the low-country. It becomes much scarcer above 2,500 feet elevation , and is rather a rarity at Haldummulla. A native collector once brought me a specimen said to have been caught at Ohiya (6,000 feet). Though mainly a jungle fly, it sometimes appears in open country, and I have noticed it once in the Fort at Galle, and it is common in the town of Jaffna.

I have two specimens from Mannar (January—wet season). They are very small, but have an exceptional amount of black, the post-discal spot being joined by a black line to the black on the terminal margin; one of these specimens also shows a very fine black marginal line on the lower wing. With these exceptions, I have noticed very little variation.

It is the slowest flying butterfly I know, and is nearly always found fluttering low on the edge of the jungle, so is very easy to catch. It flies all the year round.

146. DELIAS EUCHARIS. Found also in India and Burma.

It is abundant everywhere, at all elevations, and flies all the year round.

The larva feeds on *Loranthus*, but wanders some distance to pupate, as the pupa, which is very conspicuous, may be found anywhere, on bungalow walls, rocks, etc

It usually flies rather high, but comes readily to flowers, especially *Duranta*. It is not given to settling on wet roads, like the next species (*P. sita*).

The female varies greatly in the width of the black markings, and I have also taken two or three specimens of a variety in which the white of the upper surface is replaced by yellow. I have found this form rare, but a native collector assures me that he has frequently seen it in the Ratnapura District, so it is apparently a wet season form.

147. PRIONERIS SITA. Also found in Southern India.

A well-known mimic of the last (*D. eucharis*). The male can be distinguished by their stronger flight, their much more pointed fore wings, and the absence of the post-discal band on the upper side of the fore wing. The real mimicry is, as I believe is always the case among Ceylon butterflies, shown by the female. She has a much slower flight than the male, the fore wing is not so pointed, and the post-discal band is almost as well marked as in *eucharis*, the resemblance being even greater on the wing than in the cabinet. On the under side the mimicry is not quite so perfect; the marginal spots on the hind wing being vermilion instead of carmine, and they are broadest at the margin, whereas in *eucharis* they come to a point there. Seitz, in his work on Butterflies, states that *eucharis* is white at the apex of the fore wing below and *sita* is yellow. *D. eucharis* is yellow at the apex below, as stated by Moore, in almost all Ceylon specimens; I have, so far, only caught two which were white. All my *sita* are yellow.

The male is common all the year round at Haldummulla, especially during the south-west monsoon, and may be seen day after day in the same place. It flies fast and high, going round the same trees for hours, often in company with *eucharis*, but it comes to flowers, especially *Lantana*, early in the morning, and often settles on wet patches on the roads in the heat of the day, so it is not difficult to procure. The female is very seldom seen, or, if seen, is mistaken for ♀ *eucharis*.

I once came on females in numbers settled on an evil-smelling blossom in the Amherst gap, Uda Pussellawa, in company with *H. remba*, but not a specimen was perfect.

I have taken it from 500 to 6,000 feet elevation in Uva, and have specimens from Uda Pussellawa, Balangoda, and the hills above Ratnapura.

148. CATOPSILIA CROCALE, B., E. *Catopsilia catilla*, M.

149. CATOPSILIA POMONA, E. *Catopsilia crocale*, M., B.

Also found in India, Malaya, and Australia,

Bingham treated these as one species, but Bell has found that their larvæ are distinct. They can be distinguished as follows:—

Crocale.—A conspicuous reddish pearl-centered spot at the end of the cell on the under side of both wings. Antennæ plum coloured.

Pomona.—The spots at the end of the cell usually absent in the ♂, and absent or inconspicuous in the ♀. Antennæ blackish-brown.

C. crocale ♂ varies very little. The ♀ has two forms: one sulphur-yellow, and the other cream colour. The first is by far the most common. Var. *catilla* is the variety of ♀ *crocale*, with large reddish blotches in the centre of the under side of both wings. This variety is almost invariably sulphur-yellow in Ceylon, the only cream coloured specimen I have yet seen was at Haldummulla in November, 1919.

C. pomona ♂ varies in the amount of yellow on the upper side. The ♀ is very variable in ground colour and the amount of the black markings. I have no specimens of as bright a sulphur-yellow as normal ♀ *crocale.*

Both species appear in enormous numbers in the flight, but are not usually at their maximum at the same time. These flights of *crocale* will be found almost always to consist of well-grown specimens of 2 inches to 2½ inches in expanse. In *pomona*, on the contrary, dwarfs of under 2 inches form the great majority.

150. CATOPSILIA PYRANTHE. Found also in India and Malaya. Moore divided this into *pyranthe*, *ilea*, and *chryseis.*

It is very plentiful at times everywhere, but chiefly so at a low elevation. It seldom appears at Haldummulla, except during the north-east monsoon flights, but I have often seen it laying its eggs then. This district is exceptionally well stocked with small insectivorous birds, and I fancy the great majority of the larvæ fall a prey to them. To observe this better I have grown the food plant in a flowerpot in my garden, and though I have watched a large number of eggs being laid, I have so far failed to find a single half-grown larva on the plant.

It is very variable, but all the varieties grade. The one named *chryseis* by Moore is by far the rarest.

151. CATOPSILIA FLORELLA, B. and E. *Catopsilia gnoma*, M. Found in Africa, Persia, Afghanistan, Siam, China, etc.

C. florella differs mainly from *pyranthe* in the terminal border of the fore wing; *pyranthe* has a *continuous* band, broad at the apex and narrowed posteriorly; *florella* has a narrow *macular* band, as broad in interspace 2, as at the apex.

The difference is only clearly shown in the females.

The female is occasionally very plentiful in Ceylon, and is found in company with *pyranthe* from Galle to Jaffna. I am uncertain if I can always distinguish the male from *pyranthe*, as it seems to grade perfectly. The female is certainly very distinct on the upper side, but typical specimens of ♀ *pyranthe* may be found with the under side coloured almost as in *florella*. The antennæ of *florella* are said to be plum coloured, and those of *pyranthe* dark-brown, but I have not found this test reliable. Personally I suspect it to be only a seasonal variety of *pyranthe*, but I hope to induce a ♀ to lay her eggs in captivity and so settle the point. Breeding experiments by Mr. O. S. Wickwar and the late Colonel Manders seem to prove that *gnoma* is a wet season form of *pyranthe*, but I am not certain that *gnoma*=*florella* in this case.

It is commonest at Haldummulla in November and December, viz., during the north-east monsoon flights.

152. TERIAS LIBYTHEA, B. *Terias drona*, M.; *Terias* (*Kibreeta*) *libythea*, E. Found also in India and Burma.

This is a most variable insect in size, shape of the wings, and markings, and I consider that the variation is seasonal, the extremes being the cold and warm season forms respectively. They grade perfectly into one another. See Plate 3, figs. 1 and 2.

In the cold season form the apex of the fore wing is acuminate, the black marginal band on the fore wing is interrupted by a narrow yellow patch in interspace 1. The band on the lower wing is broken up into a broad apical patch reaching to interspace 5, followed by triangular spots at the ends of veins 2 to 5, continued a little way up each vein. There is usually a pink border to the under side of the costa of the fore wing, and the cilia are sometimes salmon-pink, as given by Bingham. In the warm season form the apex of the fore wing is more rounded, and the black marginal band on both wings is unbroken, being continuous from the apex of the fore wing to the tornus of the hind wing. The pink border to the under side of the costa is never present, and the cilia are pale yellow mixed with black. On the under side of the fore wing there is occasionally a distinct narrow pre-apical black streak running from the costa to vein 4. All the other markings are more obscure.

The cold season form is rare, and is most likely to be taken at Haldummulla from January to March, a cool, dry season following the rains. The warm season form is very plentiful here all the year round, and is found everywhere on the patanas of Uva from 500 to over 6,000 feet elevation. It is common at Galaha, near Kandy.

The size of my specimens varies from 26 to 45 mm. in expanse, dwarfs being by far the commonest. I have one specimen in which the ground colour is almost white.

153. TERIAS VENATA CINGALA with f. RAMA. *Terias cingala* and *rama*, M.; *Terias* (*Nirmula*) *venata*, E.

T. venata is found in India, China, the Philippines, etc. Moore separated this into *cingala* and *rama*, and, taking extreme examples, the difference is considerable, especially in the females. *Cingala* has the apex of the fore wings rounded, *rama* has it acuminate. Other differences are:—

In *cingala* ♂.—Upper side: The black border of the fore wing is but slightly, if at all, narrowed below vein 1, and it is *continued as a fine black line the whole length of the dorsum to the base;* its inner edge is very slightly produced inward along veins 2 and 3; there is a distinct black streak on the disco-cellulars, and the veins of the upper half of the wing are marked out in black; the sex mark is large.

Under side: All markings are very indistinct; on the fore wing there is usually a minute black spot at the upper apex of the cell, and others at the end of each vein, but all these are sometimes absent. The discal bands on the hind wing, though faint, can almost always be distinguished.

In *rama* ♂.—Upper side: The black border of the fore wing is abruptly narrowed below vein 1, and is not continued along the dorsum; its inner edge is strongly produced inwards along veins 2 and 3; there is no disco-cellular streak, and the veins are not marked out in black; the sex mark is smaller.

Under side: There is a distinct black linear spot at the upper apex of the cell. On the lower wing there is a black spot in the basal half of 7, and a series of three dusky spots across the wing near the middle of the cell. The discal bands are very clearly marked.

In *cingala* ♀.—Upper side: The black border of the fore wing is of nearly even width from vein 4 to the tornus, and it is usually produced a short distance along the dorsal margin; on the hind wing it is broad at the apex, but narrows *gradually* to the tornus; there is a fine black line on the disco-cellulars of the fore wing.

In *rama* ♀.—Upper side: The ground colour is much brighter; the black border of the fore wing is broken below vein 2, and continued to the tornus as a fine line; on the lower wing there is a broad apical black patch, but it narrows *abruptly* in interspace 5, and is continued thence to the tornus as a narrow black line; there is no mark on the disco-cellulars of the fore wing.

Under side: In *cingala* it resembles the ♂. In *rama* it answers nearly in ground colour and markings to Bingham's description of *T. læta*, wet season form.

The males are fairly constant, but it is possible to grade them. The females are very variable, and grading is easy. I believe that *rama* is the cold and *cingala* the warm weather form of our Ceylon race. The differences between them coincide very nearly to the seasonal variations of *T. libythea*. See Plate 3, figs. 1 to 6.

Cingala is very plentiful on the Uva patanas, from 500 to 3,000 feet elevation; *rama* is not so common, and is chiefly found from 3,000 feet upwards, at Haputale, Ohiya, etc. I found *cingala* very plentiful at Galaha, near Kandy. Although I have always regarded *cingala* as by far the commonest form, it is curious that the Colombo Museum did not possess a specimen till I sent them some a few years ago. They had, however, a very fine series of *rama*.

I have an exceptionally large specimen of *cingala* ♀ in which the ground colour is nearly white.

The next group of *Terias* have always given a lot of trouble, as the species have a wide range, and are very variable. Moore split it into seven species in Ceylon, viz., *hecabe*, *hecabeoides*, *simulata*, *citrina*, *uniformis*, *rotundalis*, and *templetonii*. Manders and De. Nicéville (A List of the Butterflies of Ceylon) reduced the number to three: *hecabe*, *silhetana*, and *sari*. Bingham and Evans do not give *silhetana* from Ceylon; the former allows us *hecabe* and *sari*, and the latter *hecabe* and *an der soni*.

Mr. E. E. Green, writing in "Spolia Zeylanica," Vol. VIII., Part XXX., gives *silhetana* and *hecabe*, and distinguishes them as follows:—

"*hecabe*.—Outer margin of fore wing entire; marginal area of costa distinctly black; lower extremity of black border not subtended by yellow.

"*silhetana*.—Outer margin of fore wing distinctly crenulate; marginal area of costa yellow; lower extremity of black border partially subtended by yellow."

My objection to this is that I have several *hecabe* in which the basal half of the costal border is yellow, and *silhetana* in which it is black. In a variety of *silhetana* mentioned later it is almost always black.

Bingham separates the Indian species as follows:—

Three spots in base of cell = *silhetana* or *moorei*.

Two spots in base of cell = *hecabe*.

One spot in base of cell = *andersoni* or *sari*.

My objection to this is that one or both of the spots in *hecabe* are frequently obsolete in Ceylon specimens.

My own opinion is that we have three species in Ceylon, which, making use of both Green's and Bingham's tables, I would define as follows:—

Three spots in basal half of cell; terminal margin of fore wing distinctly crenulate; lower extremity of black border of fore wing usually subtended by yellow = *silhetana*.

Not more than two spots in cell; if only one, it is usually rather indistinct; terminal margin of fore wing entire; lower extremity of black border of fore wing never subtended by yellow = *hecabe*.

One very distinct black streak in cell; terminal margin of wing entire, or very slightly crenulate; lower extremity of black border of fore wing distinctly subtended by yellow = *rotundalis*.

154. TERIAS HECABE. Found in India, Malaya, China, etc.

Moore also gives *hecabeoides* and *simulata*, but these are now regarded as varieties only. It is very variable in markings and in size, and a dwarf form from 25 to 30 mm.

in expanse is very common at Haldummulla.

While in the Northern Province in November, 1915, and January, 1916 (wet season), I noticed that a large number of specimens showed exceptionally few markings on the under side. I caught many with both spots in the cell wanting, others with only one spot, and even a specimen with two spots on one wing and none on the other. More than half of those I caught were abnormal. I have subsequently found similar varieties plentiful at Haldummulla, Kottawa, etc. On the upper side the markings are normal, but the colour of the females is rather paler than usual, the under side of the hind wing being, as a rule, very pale. There are two specimens in the Colombo Museum labelled *T. sari*, which are, I believe, only this variety of *hecabe*. They are very unlike Indian specimens of *sari*.

It is one of the commonest butterflies everywhere in the Island, and both wet and dry season forms fly together all the year round.

The colour is much affected by cyanide; specimens which have been kept too long in the killing bottle are often changed to deep orange.

155. TERIAS SILHETANA. Moore gives *citrina*, *uniformis*, and *templetonii*. From the illustrations the two former are clearly only varieties of *silhetana*, and the latter is described as having three spots in the cell. Also found in India, Burma, and Malaya.

It is as common as the last in the hills, but less plentiful in the low-country. I have taken it all over the southern half of the Island, but not so far in the north. When *Albizzia moluccana* was first planted through the tea it became a pest, but latterly its natural enemies have kept it fairly well in check. The best way to get fine specimens and varieties is to find an *Albizzia* leaf of which all the soft part has been eaten, and the pupæ are hanging about an inch apart along the ribs. Thirty to forty pupæ may be found on one leaf, and a fine series of varieties will probably hatch out, as the wet and dry season forms fly together. These pupæ on *Albizzia* leaves are always black, but a few larvæ sometimes descend and pupate on the under side of tea leaves; these pupæ are usually green.

It is extremely variable and cream-coloured specimens are not at all rare. With one possible exception mentioned below, every specimen I have seen had three spots in the basal half of the cell. but Manders mentioned one in his notes in which the basal spot was "almost obsolete." There is a form which I believe to be only a variety found in the wettest forests, the male of which was described by Moore as *rotundalis* ♂, probably because it is usually found in company with that species. It differs from normal *silhetana* in the narrower and more intense black borders to both wings, that on the fore wing being usually continued to the base of the costa, and that on the hind wing being clearly defined, never diffuse, as usual in *silhetana*. The reddish-brown apical patch, when present, is a narrow streak from the costa to vein 4, as in *hecabe*. There are three basal spots in the cell. On the lower wing below there is a black streak across the angle at the base of vein 8, which I find in all my *silhetana*, but never in *hecabe* or *rotundalis*.

Mr. A. C. Hayley has given me a specimen, which I believe to be an aberration of *silhetana*. The spots in the basal half of the cell have coalesced into one large irregular figure, and the black streak across the angle of vein 8 on the hind wing is wanting.

156. TERIAS ROTUNDALIS, M. Occasionally plentiful in forests in the wettest zone, but rare elsewhere. Mr. Mackwood, who is by far the greatest authority on our butterflies, has always insisted on its claim to specific rank. See Plate 3, figs. 7 and 8.

At the first glance the upper side of the ♂ is very like a variety of *silhetana*, but its rounded wings distinguish it. On the under side of the fore wing there is only one very dark streak in the basal half of the cell. It answers nearly to Bingham's description of *andersoni*, but in the specimens I have examined the inner margin of the black border of the fore wing is very rarely angulated on vein 7, and the ground colour of the under side is not noticeably paler than that of the upper. Moore's figures of the under side, and of what he calls the female, are fair. That of the male is, I believe, that of a variety of *silhetana*. The female resembles the male in the shape and markings of the fore wing, but is paler in colour. The border of the hind wing is a very fine black line, widening out into slightly diffuse triangular spots at the end of each vein. This border is sufficient to distinguish the female from any other Ceylon *Terias*. The types are in the British Museum. The female is what I call *rotundalis*: the male is the variety of *silhetana*, which I have described in the previous article.

The reddish apical patch below is wanting, its place being sometimes taken by an indistinct patch of black scales. Judging from my specimens, this species varies less than any *Terias* in Ceylon.

Evans writes: "*sari* is recorded from Southern India and Ceylon; the only specimens in the British Museum marked as such are two from Ceylon, which may be *andersoni*, but are certainly not *sari*." These are what I call *rotundalis*, and are now placed under that name.

Pending a decision as to whether this is *andersoni*, or a race thereof, I retain Moore's name.

I have taken it at Wellawaya and Buttala in the low-country of Uva, and have specimens from Kandy, but it is apparently only plentiful at Ratnapura and in other very wet forests.

157. IXIAS PYRENE CINGALENSIS, E. *Ixias cingalensis*, M. *Ixias pyrene* var. *cingalensis*, B. Moore also gives *pirenassa*, under which name he describes the dry season form. It is said to be peculiar to Ceylon, but is very near *pyrene*, from which it differs in having the ground colour of the fore wing extended into the base of interspace 3. This seems to be constant, though very variable in amount. I have received specimens labelled Madras and Bangalore which seem to be identical with *cingalensis*.

The males vary chiefly in the width of the black border of the hind wing and the amount of markings on the under side. The females vary in the same way, but the band on the fore wing also varies much in width and colour. In specimens from the north this band is usually yellow or pale orange, in those from the south it is almost always deep orange. In Ceylon the ground colour of the female is, I believe, always yellow, slightly paler than that of the male.

It is an insect of the dry low-country, but in some years it joins in the flights in November-December, and may then be found anywhere. I have known it then common at Haldummulla, Peradeniya, and Galle, none of which places are its usual haunts. It is very plentiful in the low-country of Uva and at Anuradhapura, but becomes rarer in the Northern Province. It is not easy to catch, as it is usually found among thorny bushes, and dives into them to escape. The female is especially hard to procure in good condition. The males sometimes settle on wet patches on the roads or in river-beds.

158. IXIAS MARIANNE. Also found in India.

Its habitat is much the same as that of the last, but it prefers more open country, and is commoner in the Northern Province. It is very plentiful in the Jaffna and Mannar Districts. It flies more away from the thorny bushes, and is therefore much easier to catch. I have never seen it settling on wet patches on the roads. I have once only seen a specimen at Haldummulla during the flights, and, in my opinion, it does not "flight."

The male varies very little, but in the female the black inner border to the orange band is sometimes missing between veins 2 and 4, and the ground colour of the under side varies greatly.

A melanism of the ♂ of this species, captured by myself in the Hambantota District, is described and figured in "Spolia Zeylanica," Vol. IX., Part XXXIII.

159. COLOTIS (IDMAIS) AMATA, B., *Idmais modesta*, M.; *Colotis amatus*, E. Also found in Africa, Persia, Arabia, and India.

It is not common in the Province of Uva, except near the boundaries of the Southern and Eastern Provinces. I have taken a single specimen at Wellawaya. It is very plentiful in the drier districts, especially in the Southern Province from Tangalla to Hambantota, and at Anuradhapura, Jaffna, Mannar, etc.

The males vary little, but the females grade perfectly from salmon colour to almost pure white, specimens as dark as the males being by far the rarest; they also vary considerably in the ground colour of the under side.

They fly slowly near the ground, and settle frequently, so are very easy to catch.

160. COLOTIS (IDMAIS) FAUSTA TRIPUNCTA, B. *Idmais tripuncta*. M.; *Colotis (Madais) fausta fulvia*, E. Also found in India. It differs from *fausta* in having three apical spots only.

Moore figures the female the same colour as the male, but all the specimens I have seen have been white. The markings are the same in both sexes, so, if a salmon-coloured female exists, she could only be distinguished by the different shape of the dorsal margin of the fore wing and the absence of the sex mark, which is a small oval patch of specialized scales on the under side of the fore wing above the basal half of vein 1.

It is found only in the north of the Island and is never plentiful. It has a very strong flight in the middle of the day in bright sunshine, but is easier to catch in the early morning. I have taken a few males at the blossom of *Cadaba indica*. It seems to frequent forest country more than any other member of the group, with the exception of *amata*.

There is a fair amount of seasonal variation, but the dry season forms, especially of the female, seem to be very rare.

I have specimens from Puttalam (October), Murunkan (July and November), and Elephant Pass (November to January), and I saw a fair number from the train near Madhu Road, on the Mannar line, in November.

161. COLOTIS (CALLOSUNE) ETRIDA LIMBATA, B., E. *Callosune limbata*, M. Peculiar to Ceylon, but is an insular race of the Indian *C. etrida*. It varies considerably, but the race seems to be well established everywhere, except in the Mannar District, where specimens that are very close to typical *etrida* may be taken in company with typical

limbata. Their flight is so weak that it is difficult to imagine specimens of *etrida* crossing by Adam's Bridge, so they may only be extreme dry season forms of *limbata*; they are almost invariably very dwarfed. (My specimens vary from 21 to 32 mm. in expanse.) In this connection I may mention that I have taken a specimen of *limbata* on the cart road at Haldummulla, at least 50 miles from its usual haunts. I believe in this case that the insect had pupated on a Hambantota salt cart, and hatched out on the road to Haputale. Specimens might, therefore, be easily brought over from India in a similar manner on the native boats, and thus interfere with the complete establishment of the race in the Mannar District.

It is found all round the north and east coasts from Chilaw to Tangalla, but its range does not, as a rule, extend for as much as 10 miles inland. The largest and darkest specimens are found in the Hambantota-Tangalla District. It flies close to the ground, and is very easy to capture.

162. COLOTIS (CALLOSUNE) EUCHARIS. Also found in India.

Confined to the north of the Island and never found very far from the sea. It is very abundant in places in the Mannar and Jaffna Districts, especially near Giants Tank.

Both sexes are very variable, and the variation seems to be largely dependent on season. In the dry season form of the male the black is confined to an external border to the orange patch on the fore wing, and very minute spots at the end of the veins on the hind wing. In the wet season form there is a large black patch on the fore wing below the orange, extending to the tornus, another small one on the costa at the commencement of the orange, and traces of an inner border connecting the two. The black spots on the hind wing are much larger, and sometimes coalesce to form a black border. In the females the orange spots at the apex vary in number from 3 to 5, 4 being the usual number; the orange often extends into the wing within the inner border of the black area. In some specimens the apical spots are nearly white. This may be the result of fading as the majority of those I have caught were worn specimens. I have, however, failed to produce the effect by exposing dead specimens to sunlight for some weeks. The under side of both sexes varies greatly in ground colour and markings.

In bright sunshine its flight is rather fast, though low, and owing to the thorns it is not easy to catch. In cloudy weather it flies little, and, if beaten up, is easily taken.

163. COLOTIS (CALLOSUNE) DANÆ, B. Moore also gives *sanguinalis*, which is only the small dry season form. Also found in India and Persia.

I have never seen it out of the Northern Province, though I believe it has been taken at Puttalam. It is extremely plentiful in the Mannar District, and is not rare at Kankesanturai on the Jaffna coast. The females are usually much scarcer than the males, but I found them in profusion at Murunkan in July.

It flies with *C. eucharis*, and has the same habits, its flight in bright sunshine being rather fast, but it is easy to catch in the early morning or in cloudy weather. Both species congregate round bushes of *Cadaba indica*, which is apparently the chief food plant of their larvæ in Ceylon, and they may be found roosting at the foot of these bushes in the evening, and the finest specimens can be easily selected.

It seems to vary much less in Ceylon than either *eucharis* or *limbata*, the chief variation being in the ground colour of the under side. Dry season specimens are very often dwarfed.

164. ANAPHÆIS MESENTINA TAPROBANA, B., E. *Belenois taprobana*, M. Peculiar to Ceylon, but is an insular race of *A. mesentina*, which is found from Africa to India.

It is very variable, but seems to be well established as a race, except in the north of the Island. I have single specimens from Jaffna and Mannar, and have seen one from Anuradhapura, which are very near typical *mesentina*, though the under side of the hind wing is chrome-yellow in all. It is much given to "flighting," especially during the north-east monsoon. During these flights it is common at Haldummulla, Colombo, Kandy, and Galle, which are much further from its normal haunts than the distance across Adam's

Bridge, so it is easy to understand the introduction of fresh blood, from the parent species, in the north.

It is very plentiful in the drier parts of the Island, especially in the Hambantota and Mannar Districts. The cream-coloured variety of the female is commonest in the wet season, in the South-East of the Island.

165. APPIAS (HYPOSCRITIA) INDRA NARENDRA, B., E. *Hiposcritia narendra*, M. Also found in S. India.

I have never come across this butterfly, my only specimen being a male from Ratnapura given to me by Mr. Mackwood. It is also found in the Knuckles District and North Matale. The material is so limited that it is impossible to say whether our Ceylon form is entitled to rank as a race, or species.

166. APPIAS (CATOPHAGA) VENUSTA, M. *Appias albina*, B.; *Catophaga albina venusta*, E. Also found in India, Burma, Malaya, etc.

Moore divides it into *venusta* and *neombo*. I have never seen anything at all resembling his figure of *neombo* ♂, but those of the female and under side are clearly lightly marked varieties of *venusta*. It is, however, curious that he describes *neombo* as extremely plentiful, and *venusta* as having been taken only at Vavuniya. In both the white and yellow varieties of the female specimens may be captured in which the pre-apical black band on the under side of the fore wing is obsolete, except for a round spot in interspace 3. This variety, however, grades perfectly into the normal.

The male can be distinguished from the next (*A. paulina*) by its more pointed wings. The female can be distinguished by having the outer margin of the black band on the under side of the fore wing irregularly zig-zag, never regularly curved as in *paulina* ♀. It has in addition, as a rule, four or five white spots at the apex of the fore wing above, while *paulina* has almost invariably only 3; but I have specimens of *venusta* in which these spots are reduced to two, those in interspaces 3 and 4 being obsolete.

It is very plentiful everywhere during the flights, but is not often found at high elevations, except when these are on.

167. APPIAS (CATOPHAGA) APULINA, B. *Catophaga melania paulina*, E. Also found in Malaya, Siam, and Java.

Moore divides it into *galene* and *lankapura*. In *galene* ♀ the under side of the hind wing is pearly white, while in *lankapura* ♀ it is yellow. They are now regarded as varieties only.

It is very variable. In heavily marked specimens of the male the costa and apex of the fore wing are heavily irrorated with black scales. This dark area is widened on the termen in interspace 3, and then narrowed abruptly, stopping before vein 1. On the hind wing there are black spots on the termen at the end of each vein, and the tornus is irrorated with black scales. In the lighter marked specimens the black scaling is restricted to the costa, and a small patch at the apex of the fore wing. The female varies much in the width of the apical black area, and in the colour and markings of the under side. The variations may be seasonal, but all varieties fly together at all times.

It is extremely plentiful all over the Island during the flights, and single specimens may be found everywhere all the year round.

168. APPIAS LIBYTHEA. Also found in India.

This is another most variable species, especially in the case of the females. In the males the variation seems to be largely dependent on locality, the darkest specimens being most often found in the south-east of the Island, in the Hambantota-Tangalla country. This does not, however, apply to the females, as the most extreme forms always fly together, and my lightest and darkest specimens were taken on the same day at Murunkan (Mannar District) in July—dry season.

The male is very similar to *A. venusta* ♂, but can be distinguished by the absence of the yellow tint on the under side of the hind wing. This is usually pure white and unmarked, but there is sometimes a small yellow patch at the humeral angle. I have two specimens which have black spots at the ends of the veins of the hind wing above; on the under side there are diffuse black spots at the ends of veins

2 and 3 of the fore wing, the terminal halves of the veins on the hind wing are very lightly marked with grayish-black, and there is a narrow gray marginal line at the tornus.

It is normally an insect of the dry low-country, but it often joins in the November-December flights, and may then be found at any elevation. I received a very dark variety of the female from Ohiya (6,000 feet) in October, 1917, before the flights had started. It was in perfect condition, not like those that have "flighted" far; it may, therefore, occasionally breed in the hills.

I have found it especially abundant in the Hambantota District in March and May, and in the Mannar country in July, November, and January.

169. APPIAS HIPPO TAPROBANA, B. *Appias taprobana*, M.; *Appias lyncida taprobana*, E. Moore also gives *A. vacans*, which is only a lightly marked variety.

Bingham separates the race *taprobana* from Southern India and Ceylon, from *hippo*, by the tact that, on the under side ot the hind wing, the sub-costal vein and veins 6, 7, and 8 are conspicuously edged with black in *taprobana*, whereas they are yellow in *hippo*. This does not apply to all Ceylon specimens, as, in my experience, almost 25 per cent. show no signs of this black edging. The width of the black border to the hind wing below is extremely variable, and specimens in which this border is narrow (viz., *A. vacans*) seldom show any black edging to the veins. All varieties fly together.

I have been collecting in Ceylon for twenty-seven years before I caught a specimen of this butterfly. In May, 1916, I saw a fair lot of males while travelling from Galle to Tangalla. After entering the dry zone east of Tangalla I saw no more, although species of *Capparis*, which is said to be its food plant, are plentiful between Tangalla and Hambantota, and much scarcer further west. It continued to be plentiful at Tangalla till, at any rate, the end of October, and I also received specimens from Kandy in September and October. It was fairly common round Galle in July, 1918, especially at Gintota, where I saw numbers flying round a tree of *Cratæva roxburghi*, on which I also found the larvæ.

170. HEBOMOIA GLAUCIPPE AUSTRALIS, B., E., *Hebomoia glaucippe*, M. Also found in Southern India, but is only a race of *H. glaucippe*, from which it differs in having no inner black border to the orange patch on the fore wing. Females in the wet season sometimes show this black border fairly well, and the ground colour of the upper side is then pale greenish-yellow instead of white.

It is very common in the low-country, especially in the drier regions. Single specimens apparently "flight" all the year round, and may be seen at the highest elevations. These fly very fast and seldom settle, so are almost impossible to catch. The largest flight I ever saw was in November, 1912. From south of Maho to Ambanpola, on the Northern line, the train passed for nearly half an hour through a swarm of many thousands.

In the dry low-country the males settle in numbers on wet patches on the roads, in river-beds, etc., and are easy to catch. The females may be taken at flowers. When settled the resemblance to a dead leaf is very striking.

171. HUPHINA NERISSA EVAGETE, E. *Huphina phryne*, M.; *Huphina nerissa*, var. *phryne*, B.

Moore also gives *H. zeuxippe* from Ceylon, but this is only a pale variety, which I have taken at Haldummulla and in the north of the Island. It is probably a dry season form.

Evans does not give *nerissa* as found in India. He gives the race *phryne* from Nepaul and Assam, and *evagete* for the rest of India and Ceylon. Bingham gives *nerissa* for Nepaul, Assam, and Bengal, and var. *phryne* from Nepaul, Bengal, Southern India, and Ceylon.

It is very plentiful in the low-country, especially in the drier parts, and may be seen settled in hundreds on mud or wet sand. It flights at least twice a year, and is then common everywhere in the hills. I have seen it in swarms at Nuwara Eliya. I have not yet, however, observed it in the Galle District.

172. HUPHINA NADINA REMBA, B. *Huphina remba*, M.; *Huphina nadina cingala*, E. Evans gives our Ceylon race

as distinct from *remba* of Southern India. Bingham says: " Ceylon specimens differ in the relative width of the black markings, and in the general paleness and dull tint of the greenish-yellow on the under side." Among the few specimens that I possess there is great variation in both respects, those from Ratnapura being much larger and far brighter in colour on the under side than those from the hills of Uva. I have, however, not yet seen a female from Ratnapura. In some of my specimens of both sexes from above 4,000 feet elevation, the greenish tint is entirely absent, all markings on the under side being in dull shades of brown. This is a dry season form. A specimen in the Colombo Museum has the under side bright brownish-red. It is not labelled with the locality, but from its size and brightness of colouring is evidently from the wet zone.

It is usually a great rarity. In February and March, 1902, it appeared in fair numbers on the bridle road from Haldummulla to the Horton Plains and at Ohiya (6,000 feet). In March, 1906, I found it plentiful at the Amherst gap, Uda Pussellawa, but every specimen was worn. On these two occasions the females seemed almost as common as the males. They flew slowly and settled frequently, so were easy to catch. The low-country form on the other hand is said to be very hard to catch, and females are extremely rare.

173. PARERONIA VALERIA CEYLONICA. *Pareronia ceylonica*, B., E.; *Nepheronia ceylonica*, M.

Moore divides it into *ceylonica*, *fraterna*, and *spiculifera*. Bingham says it differs from *pingasa* in having the black border of the hind wing of even width throughout, not narrowed towards the tornus.

In the British Museum collection *pingasa*, *spiculifera*, *ceylonica*, and *fraterna*, all stand as races of *valeria*. I consider *spiculifera* and *fraterna* are only varieties of the race *ceylonica*.

Both sexes are very variable, and extreme forms of the male are very distinct. These are named by Moore:—

1st, *ceylonica*.—The terminal margin of the fore wing is

very slightly concave, if at all. It has a very broad black border, with only a few minute, or no, blue spots on it.

2nd, spiculifera.—Smaller and of a paler blue. The termen of the fore wing more falcate, and the hind wing proportionately smaller. The black border of the fore wing is much narrower, especially near the tornus, and there is a series of small elongated blue spots on this border, that in interspace 3 being shifted inward, and the two in interspace 1 almost or quite joined to the ground colour. As Moore points out, *ceylonica* appears to be nearest to *pingasa* and *spiculifera* to *hippia*. His variety *fraterna* appears to be an intermediate form.

Ceylonica is common in the drier low-country, but is found at all elevations during the flights, but I have only taken *spiculifera* in the hills. Both are variable, and it is easy to grade them.

Personally I believe *spiculifera* to be the cold season (or high elevation) form, while *fraterna* and *ceylonica* are the dry and wet season forms respectively of those bred in the low-country. Indian writers agree in regarding *pingasa* and *hippia* as distinct species, and it is curious that varieties of our Ceylon race should almost grade into each of them. An analogous case is that of *Terias læta* and *venata*, the former of which is allied to the Ceylon *T. rama* and the latter to *T. cingala*, and yet there can be little doubt that *rama* and *cingala* are only varieties of our Ceylon race.

The females vary greatly in the width of the blue markings on the upper side and the amount of black shading below. In June, 1916 and 1917, I got specimens at Wellawaya, which were very exceptionally dark both above and below; in fact, all flying there then were of this unusual colour. The males with them seemed to be normal specimens of *ceylonica* above, but had more black shading below. I have received a similar pair from Kandy. These dark varieties of the female are good mimics of *D. septentrionis*. Normal varieties mimic *D. limniace* and *aglea*, but especially resemble *D. exprompta*, which, however, is not found in the usual haunts of *Pareronia*.

They usually fly among thorny bushes in the low-country and are not easy to catch. They are often seen at Haldummulla when "flighting," but are seldom caught, as they go fast and straight and seldom settle. The mimicry of the females also prevents recognition until too late.

Var. *ceylonica* is very common in the low-country of Uva and at Anuradhapura, but becomes scarcer further north. I have seen single specimens at Galle and Nuwara Eliya. It is not rare at Ohiya during the flights. Var. *spiculifera* is much rarer, and I have only seen it above 4,000 feet.

Papilioninæ

174. TROIDES DARSIUS. *Ornithoptera darsius*, M., E. Peculiar to Ceylon.

It differs from allied Indian species in having the yellow area on the lower wing more restricted. It varies to a certain extent in this respect, but the apex of the cell is yellow in nearly every case. I have seen about half a dozen specimens in which the whole cell was black but this variety is very rare. In a few cases the male has black spots in the yellow interspaces. One of mine has four of these spots, one each in interspaces 2, 3, 5, and 6, and the yellow in 7 is exceptionally small, the reduction being apparently caused by a spot coalescing with the basal black area. I have two others with a spot in interspace 2, and the Colombo Museum has one with spots in 2 and 3. This variety has been named *cambyses;* it is far from common.

It flies all the year round at Haldummulla, and is apparently common everywhere up to 6,000 feet elevation at least, except in the Northern Province; the furthest north that I have taken it being at Puliyankulam resthouse. It usually flies very high, but frequently visits flowers, and is then easy to catch.

175. PAPILIO (MENELAIDES) HECTOR. Also found in India.

It is very plentiful all over the low-country, but especially so in the drier districts. Single specimens visit the hills all the year round, but their flight is usually fast and straight, and they seldom settle. In the low-country they fly, as a rule, close to the ground, visiting flowers, and are very easy to catch. In November, 1914, I saw a fair number far out to sea, off the Indian and Ceylon coasts, several of which came on board the ship. At Kankesanturai, on the north coast, I have often noticed its gregarious habits when roosting for the night, a dozen or more settling on a single palmyra leaf.

The female is much more difficult to procure in good condition than the male. It can be distinguished by the much duller colour of the crimson spots and the greater amount of black on the upper surface of the abdomen.

176. PAPILIO (MENELAIDES) JOPHON. Peculiar to Ceylon, and confined to the wet zone.

I have taken it at Elpitiya and Kottawa in the Galle District, and single very battered specimens at Kegalle and Rambukkana. The latter place is, I imagine, quite its most northern limit. I am told that it is quite common at times at Ratnapura, and at Udagama and Deniyaya in the Southern Province. I have noticed very little variation, except in size.

It is very easy to catch in the early morning or late evening, but it flies very high in the middle of the day in fine weather.

177. PAPILIO (MENELAIDES) ARISTOLOCHIÆ CEYLONICA, E. *Menelaides ceylonica*, M.; *Papilio aristolochiæ*. var. *ceylonica*, B.

Peculiar to Ceylon, but is only a race of the Indian *P. aristolochiæ*.

Bingham says: "Var. *ceylonica* has a white spot at the apex of the cell of the hind wing." The great majority of Ceylon specimens show this spot, but others without it are not very rare, and are widely scattered in different localities in both the wet and dry seasons. I have one specimen, a female, from Giants Tank, Mannar, which not only has no white in the cell, but the white spots do not commence till at least 4 mm. below it. These spots are much reduced in size, the one in interspace 5 being almost obsolete. The black on the upper surface of the abdomen is much reduced.

It answers to Bingham's description of the dry season form of *aristolochiæ*. It was caught in July (dry season).

It is very common at Haldummulla all the year round, and is well distributed all over the Island from Galle to Jaffna, though it is less common in the north than in the south. Its flight is slow, and it settles frequently at flowers, so it is easy to catch. I have never noticed it "flighting."

I have seen a full-sized specimen killed and carried off for a short distance by an Asilid fly.

178. PAPILIO DEMOLEUS, B. and E. *Orpheides erithonius*, M. Found also in Arabia, Persia, India, Burma, China, etc.

It is common all over the low-country, from Galle to Jaffna, and occasionally joins the flights in great numbers, and may then be taken at the highest elevations.

The colour seems to be much affected by the sun or age, as specimens of a rusty orange are very plentiful all over the low-country, though I have never seen one over 3,000 feet elevation. These specimens will almost invariably be found to be much worn. An extraordinary aberration captured by myself on the Wellawaya-Hambantota road is figured and described in "Spolia Zeylanica," Vol. IX., Part XXXIII.

The larvæ may be found on orange and lime trees, and are very like those of *romulus*, *parinda*, and *mooreanus*, which are found on the same trees. According to Fryer ("Spolia Zeylanica," Vol. VII., Part XXVIII.), they may be distinguished as follows:—

A.—Fourth and fifth segments markedly swollen:
- *a1*.—Diagonal bands on segments 8 and 10 mainly brown, and meeting in the dorsal middle line = *mooreanus*.
- *b1*.—Diagonal bands mainly white, not meeting in middle line = *parinda*.

B.—Fourth and fifth segments not markedly swollen:
- *a2*.—Caudal tubercles white, much reduced = *romulus*.
- *b2*.—Caudal tubercles brown, size moderate = *demoleus*.

179. PAPILIO (CHARUS) MOOREANUS.

Papilio (Charus) helenus mooreanus, B., E.; *Charus helenus*, M. Peculiar to Ceylon. It is very constant and seems to deserve specific rank.

It differs from the Indian *P. helenus* in having a complete series of seven sub-discal blue lunules on the under side of the hind wing, but the two in interspaces 3 and 4 are sometimes nearly obsolete. The number of red lunules visible on the upper surface of the hind wing varies from 1 to 5 in my specimens

It is only found where there is a fairly heavy rainfall. It is very plentiful in the jungles between Haputale and Ohiya (4,000 to 6,000 feet) and occasionally descends as low as Haldummulla, but it is very rarely seen below 3,000 feet in Uva. In wetter districts it is found at very low elevations, and it has been taken at Kottawa, near Galle. It is common at Ratnapura, Madampe, and Deniyaya.

The female seems to be very rarely captured. I have only one specimen, which I bred. It differs from the male in having the inter-nervular yellow streaks on the fore wing much more clearly marked, as they are formed by scales in the ♀, and by hairs in the ♂. It also differs in having the white patch on the lower wing the same size both above and below, in the ♂ this patch is much smaller on the under surface than on the upper. The males are fond of settling on wet patches on the roads or in the beds of streams.

180. PAPILIO (ILIADES) POLYMNESTOR PARINDA, B., E. *Iliades parinda*, M. Peculiar to Ceylon, but is a race of the Indian *polymnestor*. The male differs from *polymnestor* in the greater area of the blue on the upper side. The female differs in having the blue area tinged in spots, or sometimes even entirely replaced, by pale buff. The last form is by far the rarest.

It is a most variable insect. In the male the width of the blue band on the fore wing varies greatly and the post-discal spots on the hind wing may be large and conical, as in *polymnestor*, or small and round. In the female these spots are sometimes very much reduced, and the two upper ones may be entirely obsolete.

It is very common at Haldummulla, especially during the south-west monsoon (viz., the dry season). I have seen it all over the low-country as far north as Mankulam, and I found it once in extraordinary abundance at Anuradhapura in December. The male is very fond of settling on the sand in river-beds and on wet roads in the hot weather. The female is easiest to catch when laying her eggs.

181. PAPILIO (LÆRTIAS) POLYTES ROMULUS, E. *Lærtias romulus*, M.; *Papilio polytes*, B. Evans says: "Jordan confines *polytes* to China, giving the Indian race as *romulus*."

As is well known, there are three varieties of the female: 1st, like the ♂; 2nd, mimics *P. aristolochiæ* ♀; and 3rd, mimics *P. hector* ♀. The first has been named *cyrus*, the second *polytes* or *stychius*, and the third *romulus*. The one which mimics *aristolochiæ* has usually in Ceylon a white spot in the cell (like the race *ceylonica*), but sometimes the white patch does not commence till well below it. The one which mimics *hector* is, as might be expected, a far better mimic of the female *hector* than of the male, though it is sometimes compared with the latter in articles on mimicry. It has been suggested that the crimson bodies of *aristolochiæ* and *hector* would spoil the mimicry, but in the females of both almost the whole of the upper surface of the body is black, and the abdomen is so carried in flight that the crimson would be quite invisible when viewed by a bird from above.

It joins the flights in great numbers, especially in November and December, and I have noticed that in these flights the variety which mimics *hector* is usually the commonest. At Haldummulla *hector* is far less common than *aristolochiæ*, but these flights were coming from the dry low-country, where the opposite is the case. When the flights are not on, the variety, like *hector*, is by far the rarest at Haldummulla, and the one like the male is the commonest. In the flights of November, 1919, the *cyrus* variety of ♀ was most plentiful, and the *stychius* and *romulus* varieties were in almost equal numbers. On this occasion the males rarely showed any trace of red spots below.

The males may often be found settled on mud or wet sand. The females visit flowers, but are best caught when laying their eggs. They are very easy to breed, but occasionally remain for a long time in the pupal stage Last year I had six larvæ which pupated in May. Three hatched out early in June, one at the end of July, one in the middle of August, and the last in September. The larvæ are usually to be found on orange and lime trees, but I have often seen the females laying their eggs on *Todalia aculeata*. I have bred a fair number from larvæ picked off my orange trees, but have not yet lost a single one through parasites, and I imagine their numbers must be mainly kept in check by birds.

182. PAPILIO (CHILASA) CLYTIA LANKESWARA, B. *Chilasa clytia*, var. *lankeswara*, E.; *Chilasa lankeswara*, *clytioides*, and *dissimilis*, as three species, M.

P. lankeswara has the same claim to rank as a race of *clytia* as *Euplœa asela* has to rank as a race of *core*, as it differs in the same respects.

Rothschild says that *lankeswara* "differs from *P. clytia* in the umber brown colour of the wings, and in the small sub-marginal spots of the fore wings . . . . This sub-species has been described from slightly aberrant specimens, in which the sub-marginal spots of the fore wings are partly obliterated; in most individuals the series of these spots is complete, and on such specimens Moore's *clytioides* is based."

I have only a rather poor series, but they vary much in the number and size of these spots and of the discal sagittate spots on the hind wing. The umber brown colour seems constant.

P. lankeswara is a mimic of the *Euplæas*, and it is curious that these, in Ceylon, differ from their corresponding Indian species in the same way that *lankeswara* differs from *clytia*. The form *dissimilis* mimics *D. limniace* and *aglea*, and is said to agree with Indian specimens. It varies greatly in size and the amount of the white markings. In both forms the females can be distinguished by their broader and more rounded fore wings.

It has as rapid a flight as any *Papilio* in Ceylon, but does not always make use of its powers. When visiting flowers, or hovering over wet patches on the roads, its flight is slow, and so like that of a *Danaida* or *Euplœa*, that after thirty years' experience I am still sometimes deceived by it. I imagine that protection is most needed by the female when laying her eggs; she would then probably be hovering slowly over the cinnamon, etc., and her mimicry would be most advantageously displayed. The pupa is a most wonderful example of camouflage. It is fixed to a branch so as to exactly resemble the end of a broken twig, and I have found it difficult to distinguish even in a breeding cage.

I have found *dissimilis* rather more plentiful than *lankeswara*, but neither form is common. The best localities I have noticed are the road from Wellawaya to Muppane, and Dambulla. I have also taken it at Haputale (5,000 feet), Haldummulla, and Galle, but have not yet seen it in the Northern Province.

183. PAPILIO CRINO with ♂ *f.* MONTANUS, B. *Harimala montanus*, M.; *Achillides crino fruhstorferi*, E.; *P. crino* is found in India. Evans gives *fruhstorferi* as the Ceylon race. Bingham says: "Var. *montanus*, Felder, was founded on specimens devoid of the cottony scent streaks on the upper side of the fore wing." These streaks are present in the male in a fair proportion of Ceylon specimens, but those without them are usually the commoner.

It is especially abundant in the low-country of Uva and the North-Central Province, but is common everywhere in the low-country, except in the extreme north. I have seen it once in the Mannar District. Individuals which are apparently "flighting" appear all the year round in the hills. I once saw a very big flight at Galle in March, the direction was south-west, viz., straight out to sea. It continued for three or four days, and enormous numbers must have perished in the sea.

The male is often to be found settled in numbers in the sandy river-beds, and is very easy to catch. The females are not easy to procure in good condition. They can be distinguished by the narrower green band on the fore wing, and there is also usually a diffuse orange spot near the apex of the hind wing above.

184. Papilio (Pathysa) antiphates alcibiades. *Pathysa antiphates*, M.; *Pathysa antiphates ceylonicus*, E.; *Papilio antiphates alcibiades*, var. *ceylonicus*, B.

P. antiphates is found in India, Burma, Siàm, Malaya, China, etc.

Rothschild describes *ceylonicus* as having "Two basal black bands on the upper side of the fore wing extending beyond the median nervure; the fourth band broad and reaching to the median nervure (not triangular)." This I consider merely a seasonal variety. In my two specimens from the dry zone this fourth band does not reach the median nervure, and is triangular; those from the wet zone agree with Rothschild's description. The specimens in the Colombo Museum vary much in this respect, and in one the band is very acutely triangular; unfortunately it has no label of locality. It is so rare and so variable in every respect that it is difficult to say whether it is a local race or not, but dry zone specimens seem to agree approximately with Bingham's description of *alcibiades*.

The only place where I have personally taken it is at Sirigalla, near Muppane, in the low-country of Uva. I found it settled on wet sand in the bed of a stream. A native catcher has brought me specimens from Ratnapura, Kottawa and Deniyaya. All my specimens are males.

185. Papilio (Pathysa) nomius. Also found in India.

This is usually rare in Uva, but it occasionally appears in great numbers at the commencement of the north-east monsoon. In October, 1893, I found it in hundreds settled on the wet roads near Wellawaya, and I have heard of two similar swarms in the same district since. It joins in the flights, and I have notes of its occurrence above Haldummulla at an elevation of 5,000 feet. I have also seen it in great numbers on the road from Trincomalie to Dambulla, and have received specimens from Kandy.

It varies a great deal in the width of the black markings, dry season forms being much lighter than those taken during the rains. I have not yet obtained specimens from the wet zone, though it is found there.

186. PAPILIO (ZETIDES) DOSON, M., E. *Papilio (Zetides) eurypylus jason,* B.

Evans gives *doson* as peculiar to Ceylon, with *eleius* as the S. Indian race; Bingham gives *jason* from Ceylon and S. India. Moore divides our Ceylon form into *doson* and *telephus,* he says that *doson* "differs from *Z. telephus* in being larger, the transverse medial macular band much narrower in both wings. On the under side the medial band is also narrower, especially across the hind wing . . ., the outer black spots to the discal band are larger, and less bordered with carmine." Extreme specimens are fairly distinct, but they vary, and it is easy to grade them. I consider the difference is seasonal. In March, 1917, I took *telephus* at Wellawaya after two months' drought, and *doson* in May after heavy rains.

It is extremely plentiful at times all over the low-country, except in the extreme north, and I have taken it from Kottawa to Vavuniya. It sometimes "flights" in great numbers, and on rare occasions these flights visit the hills, and specimens may then be taken at any elevation. The males settle in crowds on wet patches on the roads and in river-beds, and a dozen or two may be covered at one stroke of the net. The females seem to be very difficult to obtain, and I only possess a single specimen.

187. PAPILIO (ZETIDES) SARPEDON TEREDON, E., B. *Dalchina teredon,* M.

Also found in S. India.

It differs from *sarpedon* in the narrower medial band across both wings, and in the upper portion of this band, on the fore wing, being of a more distinct greenish shade. The width of the band varies in Ceylon specimens, but the greenish tint is usually very pronounced; in one of my specimens, however, it is almost indistinguishable.

They may be seen day after day in the same place flying very fast round the tree tops, generally in pairs, but are then extremely hard to catch. The females occasionally visit flowers, but I have found it very difficult to get specimens in good condition. The males are much addicted to settling on wet roads, but are not gregarious like *doson;* usually there is only one on the wet patch, and to find more than two is extremely rare.

They are very plentiful at Haldummulla all the year round, and I have found them common at Kottawa, near Galle, and at Ohiya (6,000 feet). They become much rarer in the drier districts, and I have not yet seen a specimen in the northern half of the Island. They do not join in the flights.

188. PAPILIO (ZETIDES) AGAMEMNON MENIDES, E. *Papilio agamemnon,* B. *Zetides agamemnon,* M.; *P. agamemnon,* is found in India, Malaya, China, etc. The race *menides,* which only differs in the greater length of the tails, is restricted to Southern India and Ceylon.

It is common all over the low-country, but especially so in the south. Not rare in the hills at times, and, as a rule, does not appear to be "flighting," as the direction of flight is seldom constant. In November, 1917, however, I saw it at Pattipola in great numbers, and on this occasion it was certainly "flighting," as all were flying due south.

It is most frequently caught when visiting flowers. It only stops a very short time at each blossom, so is not easy to capture. Occasionally the males may be taken settled on the mud near cattle sheds or lines.

HESPERIIDÆ.

I have found this group of butterflies very difficult to name, as the true status of our forms can only be arrived at by the examination of a large number of allied species from India, etc. The literature is rather meagre, as they were not dealt with in De Nicéville's work, and have not yet been reached in the "Fauna of India" series. The leading works are Moore's "Lepidoptera Indica," and "A Revision of the Oriental Hesperiidæ" by Messrs. Elwes and Edwards (Transactions of the Zoological Society of London, Vol. XIV., Part 4). The latter work mainly decides questions of specific identity by an examination of the genitalia of the males, and the authors point out "that a very considerable practice in making this examination, and great experience in estimating the value of the characters observed, are necessary to form an opinion on the subject." I confess that I have had no previous experience, but the sketches in the plates 4, 5, and 6, are in nearly every case the result of the examination of a large number of specimens. In no case was the sketch made from a single specimen. I have sent sets of my slides to the Colombo Museum and to the Indian Agricultural Institute at Pusa, where any one interested can examine them. They include all the Ceylon Hesperiidæ, with the exception of *C. spilothyrus* and *G. albofasciata*. When removed from the body and allowed to dry, the clasps often shrivel and curl up, thus entirely altering their outlines as seen under a microscope. I have, therefore, whenever possible, used perfectly fresh, undried specimens for my sketches.

In cases where there are only slight differences between the prehensores of two forms, it is advisable to examine a large number of each, to ascertain if these differences are permanent, or only casual variations.

Unfortunately my material from India has been, so far, limited to about 500 specimens, and in only a few cases have I had a good series of any one form. My experience has been that, in some genera, notably *Telicota* and *Halpe*, the species show a strong tendency to split up into local races and I am of opinion that, in these cases, the prehensores will be found a more constant and reliable guide than external colouration. I have dissected very large numbers of some Ceylon species and have always found that the variation of the prehensores is very slight.

A question which arises is whether differences in colour caused by climatic influences are accompanied by changes in the prehensores. Recent investigation seems to prove that they are. Fruhstorfer found seasonal variation in the clasps of *Nacaduba pavana*, and other instances are known. Indian writers treat *Caprona saraya* as a seasonal form of *C. ransonnettii*, though Elwes and Edwards point out that their clasps differ considerably. In Ceylon *C. siamica* shows an almost similar divergence from *C. ransonnettii*, and would therefore, I presume, be regarded as a seasonal form. I have examined over a dozen specimens of *C. siamica*, and have, so far, found no signs of grading in the clasps, and am therefore inclined to regard it as distinct till proved to be only a variety. (See Plate 4, figs. 9, 10, 11, and 12.)

Mr. T. R. Bell has an excellent article in "The Journal of the Bombay Nat. Hist. Soc.," Vol. XXVII., Part 2, dividing the *Hesperiidæ* into sub-families from the evidence of their early stages. Unfortunately he puts *Hantana infernus* into the sub-family *Achalarinæ*, and *Celænorrhinus spilothyrus* into the *Celænorrhinæ*. As I believe our form of *C. spilothyrus* is the female of *H. infernus* I am unable to make use of his divisions. I therefore follow Capt. E. Y. Watson and divide them into three, viz., 1. *Hesperiinæ*, 2. *Pamphilinæ*, and 3. *Ismeneinæ*. Mr. Bell points out that the larvæ of the 1st and 3rd of these sub-families feed on dicotyledons, while those of the 2nd feed on monocotyledons, so the division seems a natural one.

In describing external markings, Elwes and Edwards use a different nomenclature for the parts of the wing from that given in Plate 1. For instance, they call the vein next below vein 2 vein 1*a*, and the interspace between this vein and vein 2 cell 1*a*. To avoid confusion I have continued to use Bingham's terms, and call the former vein 1, and the latter interspace 1.

Hesperiinæ

189. HANTANA INFERNUS. Peculiar to Ceylon.

This is a very variable species. In my lightest marked specimen the markings on the upper side of the fore wing consist of two minute pre-apical yellow spots. In the most heavily marked there are three pre-apical spots, one spot in the cell touching the pre-costal vein, and a smaller one below it, and a small one in the centre of interspace 2. Some specimens have a minute spot on the costa, above the spot in the cell; Moore says these are females; all I have seen were males. The upper side of the hind wing is usually uniformly black, but sometimes the terminal half is irrorated with golden yellow scales shaped like a sword blade; these are grouped between the veins, forming a row of post-discal diffuse spots. On the under side of the fore wing, in addition to the pre-apical spots, there is sometimes a straight row of five spots, viz., three from the costa to the middle of the cell, a round spot in interspace 2, and a smaller one below in interspace 1. There is also occasionally a large very diffuse spot at the apex of interspace 1. On the hind wing some specimens have complete discal and post-discal rows of very diffuse orange spots; in others all these spots are absent. When present they are formed by sword-shaped scales as above.

It is usually found in jungle from 2,000 to 6,000 feet elevation, and settles with its wings spread out flat on the under side of a leaf; if disturbed it seldom flies far. It is very active in the net, and the wings rub easily, so perfect specimens are not easy to procure. I have not yet seen a female.

It is plentiful at Haputale, and not rare at Haldummulla, and occurs at all times of the year. I have also specimens from Kandy and the hills above Ratnapura. For prehensores see Plate 4, figs. 1 and 2.

190 CELÆNORRHINUS SPILOTHYRUS, E. *Plesioneura spilothyrus*, M Also found in Southern India.

Evans says: " *C. fusca* can easily be separated from *spilothyrus* by the chequered cilia." In several of my specimens the cilia of the hind wings are distinctly chequered. Elwes and Edwards point out that in *C. fusca* the costal spot "is usually, but not always, white," whereas in Ceylon specimens "it seems to be always yellow." Moore says this spot is white in the male, and yellow in the female. He may be right. In every specimen I have seen it was yellow, though varying in depth of colour, but I have never seen a male from Ceylon.

It varies greatly in the size and shape of the spots on the fore wing, and one or both of those in interspace 1 are often missing. The definition of the golden-yellow spots on the hind wing is very variable, and they may be entirely obsolete below. They are formed by sword-shaped scales identical with those of *H. infernus*, but, when especially well marked, there is also a mixture of scales of a different shape.

It is found in the same localities, and has the same habits as *H. infernus*, but, whereas the female of *infernus* seems unprocurable, in *spilothyrus* the opposite is the case, and I have not yet seen a male. This, coupled with the resemblance in habits, and scaling, gives rise to a suspicion that *infernus* is the male, and *spilothyrus* the female, of our Ceylon form. Of course, this can only be proved by breeding. The difference in venation is not more than might be expected in different sexes of the same insect.

Mr. Talbot informs me that the Hill Museum, Witley, have the specimen of *spilothyrus* which Swinhoe used to illustrate the ♂ in "Lepidoptera Indica" and it proves to be a female, like all their other specimens of *spilothyrus* from Ceylon.

My specimens are from Haldummulla, Haputale and the hills above Ratnapura.

191. SARANGESA ALBICILIA. Peculiar to Ceylon, but possibly only a race of *S. dasahara* of India It differs in having the under side of the hind wing white. The prehensores seem to be identical. (See Plate 4, figs. 13 and 14.)

It varies little. On the fore wing the discal spot in interspace 2 is sometimes obsolete. On the under side of the hind wing there is sometimes a complete series of diffuse black marginal spots in interspaces 1 to 5, in other specimens there is no trace of these.

In May, 1917, it was apparently "flighting" at Haldummulla, and I caught a fair number of specimens. The direction of flight was west. It is usually a rarity here, but is very common in the low-country of Uva. I have taken it at Trincomalie in November, and have received specimens from Kandy taken in August.

192. COLADENIA INDRANI TISSA. *Coladenia tissa*, M. *Coladenia* (*Cnaiolade*) *indrani tissa*, E.

The types are from Ceylon. It is a race (or variety) of *C. indrani*, which is found in India and Burma.

Elwes and Edwards distinguish *tissa* from *indrani* by the " distinct displacement inwards of the middle one of the three pale spots which form the sub-apical series:" In my specimens these spots vary in number from 2 to 5, though 3 is most usual. The spot in 7 is usually displaced inwards, but the displacement is sometimes very slight. All other markings and the ground colour are also extremely variable. I have only been able to examine a single specimen of *indrani* from Coorg. In it the three pre-apical spots are equal in size, and are far larger than in any specimen of *tissa* that I possess. They are arranged in a straight line. The clasp differs very slightly from that of *tissa*, but this cannot be relied on with the examination of only a single specimen. For the prehensores of *tissa*, see Plate 4, figs. 5 and 6.

It is very widely distributed in Ceylon, but I have never found it common. I have taken it at Haldummulla, Wellawaya, Hambantota, Galle, Kegalle, and Vavuniya, and have specimens from Kandy. It settles with its wings spread out flat on the under side of a leaf, and, as a rule, does not fly far if disturbed; but its flight is so rapid that it is not always easy to see where it settles.

193. TAGIADES DISTANS.

Peculiar to Ceylon, but closely allied to other forms of *obscurus*, which are found in India. *T. obscurus* is from Java.

Moore says: " *Obscurus* differs in the absence of the discal semi-transparent spots on the fore wing." Elwes and Edwards say they have not been able to compare Malayan with Ceylon specimens, but regard the distinction as of no value, as these spots are often missing in Ceylon specimens. Males without them are not rare, but all the females in my collection show them prominently. I have received several specimens of an allied form from Coorg and Kanara. They differ in many ways from Ceylon specimens, but especially in the markings on the under side of the hind wing. The clasp is distinct, though clearly allied. The clasp of *distans* is figured on Plate 4, fig. 7.

It is common from sea level up to 5,000 feet at least, wherever there is a fair rainfall. It flies all the year round, but is most abundant at Haldummulla, near the changes of the monsoons.

On the roads at Haldummulla large skippers are often met "flighting" west. When approaching they are inconspicuous, but when going away they show a lot of white. These flights are, I believe, almost entirely composed of *T. distans* and *atticus*, but one specimen I succeeded in catching proved to be *U folus*. In May, 1917, they were exceptionally numerous, and all I caught, or saw settled, were *T. distans*. When not flighting, it only flies a short distance, and settles with its wings expanded, usually on the under side of a leaf but often in the most conspicuous positions.

194. TAGIADES LITIGIOSA. *Tagiades atticus*, M. Aurivillius has discovered that the name *atticus* is wrong for this species, and *litigiosa* is the oldest name for it. Fruhstorfer names the race from S. India and Ceylon, *T. menaka vajuna*.

Also found in India, Burma, Malaya, etc.

This is a very variable species; as a rule, specimens from Kandy, Ratnapura, and other places in the wet zone are much smaller, and have less white than those from the highest elevations. The marginal spots on the hind wing vary greatly in size, but the one at the end of vein 1 is usually the largest. The black spot in the cell on the under side of the hind wing is frequently missing. In my series the number of hyaline spots on the fore wing varies from 5 to 10, the lowest one in the cell, and those in interspaces 2 to 5 being sometimes obsolete. The clasp is figured on Plate 4, fig. 8 I have noticed no variation in it so far, but have only been able to spare specimens for dissection from Kandy and Ratnapura (wet zone).

It is much rarer at Haldummulla than *distans*, and far harder to catch, as it seldom seems to settle here. It is commoner at Haputale (5,000 feet), and I am told that it is abundant in Nuwara Eliya at times, though I have so far failed to get specimens from there. I can get plenty from Kandy.

195. Tapena thwaitesi. Also found in India, Burma, Malaya, etc.

Elwes and Edwards divide this genus as follows:—

"*A*. Upper lobe of clasp bifid at the apex = *thwaitesi*.

"*B*. Upper lobe of clasp not bifid at the apex.

"*a*. Upper lobe of clasp with three limbs, all of which are serrate. Similar to *thwaitesi*, but smaller and paler above= *minuscula*.

"*b*. Upper lobe of clasp with two limbs, of which the lower is serrate and the upper simple. Size of *thwaitesi*, but upper side in the male nearly uniformly umber brown = *hampsoni*."

Swinhoe groups them all as one species, as the only differences are, he considers, in the genitalia, and it seems possible that they may eventually be only classed as local races of *thwaitesi*, in spite of the great internal differences.

I have only so far been able to dissect four specimens of our Ceylon form, and the same number from Kanara. The prehensores in both are practically identical, see Plate 4, figs. 3 and 4, and the clasps agree with Elwes and Edwards' figure of that of *hampsoni*, except that both limbs of the upper lobe are serrated. This serration of the upper limb can only usually be seen when it is wet; as it dries it curls up and the serration disappears.

Externally my specimens of both sexes closely agree with the description of *hampsoni*. The clearness of the dark markings in the male is very variable. The name *thwaitesi* was originally given to a specimen from Ceylon, so that name will stand for our form in any case, and, from the limited material at my disposal, I believe *hampsoni* from S. India to be indistinguishable.

A great rarity, and I have never personally caught a specimen. A native collector has sent me specimens from Kandy, Deniyaya, and Kottawa, and I saw Mr. Mackwood catch one at the latter place in February.

196. Caprona ransonnettii, E. *Abaratha ransonnettii* M. Also found in India.

This is a variable insect. The hyaline spots on the fore wing vary much in size and shape, the two in interspace 1, and the one at the upper margin of the cell being often nearly obsolete. In all my males there are three pre-apical spots, but the females sometimes have four or five. Some specimens have a faint marginal row of pale spots, with a sub-marginal row of more conspicuous ones in interspaces 4, 5, 6 and 7, thus disagreeing with Elwes and Edwards' classification of the species. The markings on the under side are very variable.

It is fairly common at Haldummulla during the south-west monsoon (dry season), but becomes much more abundant at a lower elevation, and I have taken it all over the low-country of Uva and at Trincomalie and Vavuniya. The males are most frequently found settled on the wet sand in river-beds or on wet roads; the females visit flowers, and seldom fly far if disturbed.

The clasps are figured on Plate 4, figs. 9 and 10.

197. CAPRONA SIAMICA? Not mentioned in any list that I know of Ceylon Butterflies, but it is very near to *C. saraya*. See Plate 2, fig. 5. Capt. Riley has compared a specimen from Ceylon with the type of *siamica* and thinks our form is wrongly named, and that it is true *saraya*.

Elwes and Edwards, in their analytical table of the genus *Caprona*, divide the species by two important characters: 1st, the possession of "a terminal row of pale spots on the fore wing above"; and 2nd, the presence of "a hyaline spot in the cell of the fore wing above, near the middle." Neither of these help to place this species. The row of pale spots is sometimes very prominent, but in other specimens it is equally obscure. The spot in the middle of the cell is usually present, but I have specimens without it. The other hyaline spots seem fairly constant, but the large one at the end of the cell is sometimes divided into two very small ones. The pre-apical spots usually number 5, but they are sometimes reduced to 3. As a rule, the under side of the hind wing is pure white, but it is occasionally tinged with ochreous. The ring of small black spots round the disc number 10 in all my specimens. In general appearance it somewhat resembles Elwes and Edwards' figure of *saraya*. Evans thinks *saraya* is a dry season form of *ransonnettii*. If he is right, it seems probable that *siamica* bears the same relationship, as the clasps differ from those of *ransonnettii* in much the same way as those of *saraya*. See Plate 4, figs. 11 and 12. They seem to be intermediate between those of *saraya* and *syricthus*.

Judging from Mr. Mackwood's note below it is caught at Kandy in the wet months, but July, August, though wet months in Kandy itself are dry months a very few miles to the North.

I found it fairly common many years ago in chenas at 1,000 to 2,500 feet elevation below Haldummulla, but I have not been able to work this country lately. It is not rare at Wellawaya, and a native collector caught fourteen specimens there at the beginning of November, 1917 (commencement of rainy season). It does not seem to settle on wet sand, like *C. ransonnettii*. I have not yet seen a female.

"A scarce fly Caught in Kandy and Haragam, January, July, August, October, and November." (F. M. Mackwood.)

198. GOMALIA ALBOFASCIATA. Originally described from Ceylon, but is also found in India.

A very scarce and local insect in Ceylon. It is said to be found in the jungle between Weerawella and Kirinde, in the Hambantota District. I have frequently searched for it there without success, but only in February, March, and April.

My only specimen was given to me by the late Mr. John Pole. It has no label of locality or date.

"Hambantota District in July. Found also near Batticaloa." (F. M. Mackwood.)

199. HESPERIA (SPIALIA) GALBA. Also found in India, Burma, etc.

This is one of the commonest skippers in Ceylon. I have taken it all over the low-country, from Galle to Jaffna, and Mr. F. M. Mackwood has taken it at Pattipola, but it is rare above 4,000 feet.

It is especially common at Haldummulla, and can be taken all the year round. Specimens from Jaffna and Mannar are usually very small.

It varies little, except in the size of the white discal band on the upper side of the hind wing. It flies low and settles on the ground or short grass, and never goes far if disturbed, so is very easy to capture.

Pamphilinæ

200. BARACUS VITTATUS. Peculiar to Ceylon.

The male varies in the size of the white patch on the fore wing, and the spots in interspaces 6 and 7 may be absent. In the female these spots are also sometimes absent, and those in interspaces 2 and 3 may be very small; the amount of white scaling on the lower wing also varies considerably.

It is exceedingly plentiful on patanas at high elevations, especially on the Horton Plains. It may occasionally be taken on grass by the roadsides as low as 3,000 feet at Haldummulla, and I found it common at Galaha, near Kandy. Those taken below 4,500 feet are usually smaller than those from the highest elevations.

For prehensores see Plate 4, figs. 15 and 16. They bear a very close resemblance to those of *B. subditus* from Coorg.

201. SUASTUS GREMIUS and *f.* SUBGRISEA. *S. gremius* is also found in India, Burma, China, etc.; *subgrisea* is confined to Ceylon.

Moore gives *subgrisea* as a distinct species and says it differs in having the three discal spots smaller, the sub-apical spots very indistinct, and the under side less gray. *S. gremius* is a most variable insect, but all my varieties grade perfectly with one exception. This specimen was taken on this estate. It is smaller than usual, and the ground colour above and below is much darker. The only markings above are two minute spots, one each in interspaces 2 and 3 of the fore wing. Below, in addition to these spots, there are very minute black dots in interspaces 6, 7, and 8 of the fore wing, and a small black spot in the cell of the hind wing; the discal series of black spots is wanting. This may be the insect named *subgrisea* by Moore, though he describes it as having the black discal spots below. I have only seen the one specimen. The ground colour of the under side of *gremius* seems to vary climatically, those from the hills being usually much darker than those from the low-country.

The larva feeds on palms, and the butterfly is found wherever coconuts are grown, and in some places where they are not. It is very abundant at Galle and Kurunegala, common at Pallai, near Jaffna, and not rare at Haputale and Haldummulla. I have no records of its capture above 5,000 feet.

For clasp of *gremius*, see Plate 4, fig. 17. That of *subgrisea* seems to be identical.

202. SUASTUS MINUTA, E. *Tagiades minuta*, M. Peculiar to Ceylon.

The prehensores are somewhat like those of *S. gremius*, the tegumen being almost identical. See Plate 4, figs. 17, 18 and 19. They are very distinct from those of any *Tagiades* that I have examined.

It is very rare in Uva, and I have never found it common anywhere; the native collectors, however, seem to be able to get any quantity at Kandy, and they have also sent me specimens from Ratnapura and Kottawa. The few living specimens I have seen only flew a short distance, and were very easy to catch.

203. IAMBRIX SALSALA, E. *Astictopterus stellifer*, M.

Found also in India, Burma, Malaya, Hong Kong, etc.

The male is fairly constant, but the female varies very much in the number and size of the translucent discal spots on the fore wing. These vary in number in my specimens from 4 to 8.

It is very common in jungles or on grass by the roadsides at Haldummulla, especially during the dry season. It is plentiful in jungles near Galle, and I have also taken it at Hambantota, Anuradhapura, Trincomalee, Kandy, etc., but have no notes of its capture above 4,000 feet, or north of Vavuniya.

204. TARACTROCERA MÆVIUS Found also in India, Burma, Borneo, etc.

Evans says: "The Ceylon form of *mævius* has not the veins on the hind wing below conspicuously pale as in continental specimens." My series vary considerably in this respect, and also in the size of the spots on the upper side which are sometimes white and sometimes yellow in both sexes.

It is very abundant at Haldummulla all the year round, and I have found it plentiful on the ramparts at Galle in May. It is so small, and looks so like a fly, that it can be easily over looked, but I fancy it is common on short grass in most districts. I have not, however, noted it yet north of Vavuniya.

205. AMPITTIA MARO. Also found in India, Burma, Malaya, China, Dutch Indies, etc.

The amount of the yellow markings is variable in both sexes, but specially so in the male.

A. maroides (De N.) is given as a distinct species. It differs from *maro* "on both sides of the fore wing in lacking the chrome yellow spot in the middle of the submedian interspace." I have a specimen from Kandy, so it is evidently only a variety in Ceylon, though it may form a local race elsewhere.

It may be seen in plenty at times in growing paddy, but I have also taken a few in the grass by the roadsides at Haldummulla during the south-west monsoon (dry season), when the paddy-fields are not being cultivated. Other localities I have noted are Kandy, Galle, and Anuradhapura, and a single specimen from Giants Tank near Mannar. It flies low and settles often, so is very easy to catch.

206. HYAROTIS ADRASTUS. Also found in India, Burma, Dutch Indies, Hong Kong, etc.

The spots on the fore wing vary much in size, and those in interspaces 1 and 3 are sometimes absent. The clasp is figured on Plate 4, fig. 20.

It is usually very rare at Haldummulla, but in July, 1900, it appeared in fair numbers in the jungle bordering this estate. They flew fast, settled rather high, and were very difficult to catch. They could, however, be found day after day in the same spot, so gave me plenty of chances. Except for a single specimen at Kottawa, I have never come across it anywhere else, so imagine it must be very local. I get plenty of specimens from the native collectors at Kandy.

207. MATAPA ARIA Found also in India, Burma, Dutch Indies, Hong Kong, etc.

This can be at once distinguished, when settled, from any other Ceylon skipper of the same size, by its bright red eyes, which, however, fade soon after death.

The only place I have taken it is at Hirimbura, 3 miles from Galle, in February, March, April, July, and October. As a rule it only flies a short distance if disturbed, and is very easy to catch. I have received specimens from Kandy and Ratnapura

The prehensores are figured on Plate 4, figs. 21 and 22.

208. GANGARA THYRSIS. Also found in India, Burma, Dutch Indies, Philippines, etc. Bainbrigge Fletcher describes it as a minor pest of palms in India ("Some South Indian Insects").

Too rare to be regarded as a pest in Ceylon and very local; the only place where I personally have seen it on the wing being Kegalle. The native collectors never sent me a specimen till August, 1918. They then caught a fair number of males at Kandy, and explained that they had only then discovered that it flew very late in the evening. In August, 1919, they had another good catch, including a few females.

The clasp is figured on Plate 4, fig. 24.

209. PADUKA LEBADEA, E. *Matapa subfasciata*, M. Also found in India, Malaya, Dutch Indies, etc.

The figure in Moore's "Lepidoptera of Ceylon" is evidently drawn from a very dwarfed specimen, as with the exception of *G. thyrsis*, it is the largest Hesperid in the Island. He also describes it as only 2 inches in expanse. It is rare and local, and

I have never seen a specimen alive. Like the last (*G. thyrsis*) it flies late in the evening, and the Kandy collectors brought me plenty in August, 1918 and 1919. The female is much rarer than the male. See Plate 2, fig. 4.

The clasp is figured on Plate 4, fig. 23.

210. UDASPES ALYSOS. *Notocrypta feisthamelii*, E ; *Plesioneura alysos*, M.

211. UDASPES RESTRICTA. *Notocrypta feisthamelii*, E.; *Plesioneura restricta*, M.

Swinhoe, in "Lepidoptera Indica," gives *N. feisthamelii* and *N. restricta* from Ceylon, and Fruhstorfer names them *Notocrypta alysos alysos* and *N. feisthamelii restricta.*

The type of *feisthamelii* is from the Moluccas, and races are found in India, Malaya, China, Japan, Philippines, etc. The types of *restricta* are from Ceylon.

The genitalia of *restricta* are difficult to distinguish from those of *Udaspes folus*. Moreover Mr. T. R. Bell says ("Journal of the Bombay Natural History Society.," Vol. XXVII., p. 786), that their larvæ are difficult to distinguish from each other, and their pupæ are quite indistinguishable. Both feed on *Zinziberaceæ*. I therefore do not see how they can be placed in different genera. *Udaspes* is an older name than *Notocrypta*.

I agree with Moore that there are two distinct species in Ceylon, and Mr. Bell has proved, by breeding, that the two corresponding forms in Kanara are distinct.

Our forms are :—1st, *alysos*.—Upper side fore wing : The white band is of nearly even width throughout, and its outer edge has a fairly regular curve. Beyond this band there is, as a rule, one spot in interspace 4, but this is sometimes absent. I have seen a few specimens in which there was also a very minute spot in interspace 5. Under side : The white band is *always* continued to the costa by an opaque whitish patch. 2nd, *restricta*.—Upper side fore wing : The white band broad in interspace 2, and narrower in the cell and interspace 1. White spots outside the band in 3, 4, 6, 7 and 8, and occasionally in 5. The spot in 6 is sometimes absent.

That in interspace 3 *is always the largest; this spot is never present in alysos.* The white band is *never* continued to the costa below.

I have examined a great number of specimens, but so far I have seen only one exception to the rule *in Ceylon*, that, if the band below is continued to the costa, there are never more than two spots beyond the band, and very rarely more than one; whereas, if it is not so continued, there are always 4 to 6. The sole exception is in the Colombo Museum collection. In addition to the small spots in 4 and 5, it has two very minute pre-apical dots in 7 and 8. I have only noticed small differences in the prehensores, the most marked being the size of the clasps. I have selected males of both for dissection approximately equal in size, and the clasp of *restricta* has invariably proved to be larger, and *comparatively broader*, than that of *alysos*. Elwes and Edwards describe *feisthamleii* as having a " broad white band on the fore wing, and five white spots besides," and quote Leech as saying that the band is continued to the costa below by a pale patch. If *both* these points are essential, typical *feisthamelii* does not, I believe, exist in Ceylon.

Both are plentiful at times at Haldummulla, though *alysos* is by far the commoner form. I have specimens of *alysos* from Kandy, Ratnapura, and Galle, and of *restricta* from Haputale and Kandy. I have bred *restricta* on *Kæmpferia rotunda*.

They are usually found in jungle, and fly rather fast up and down the paths, settling frequently. They are not at all shy, and, if frightened away, will nearly always return in a few minutes,

212. UDASPES FOLUS. Found in India, Burma, Dutch Indies, etc.

A rarity in Ceylon, though Bainbrigge-Fletcher says it is "occasionally a serious pest of ginger and turmeric" in India (" Some South Indian Insects ").

I have seen it three times in my garden, and believe it had bred on *Kæmpferia rotunda*, as I caught a freshly hatched one close to the plant, and found a fresh empty pupa case on a leaf. I have also taken it at Kirinde, in the Hambantota District, and have seen specimens from Badulla, Madulsima, and Wellawaya.

213. TELICOTA BAMBUSÆ. Found also in India, Malaya, Australia, China, etc.

It is very common at Haldummulla, and I have taken it in every month but January. It is not rare at Haputale (5,000 feet), and I have specimens from Colombo, Kandy, Galle, etc.

I have examined a fairly large number of specimens from various districts of India and find local variation in markings, usually accompanied by variation in the prehensores. In other species considerably less variation is frequently considered sufficient for the formation of new species or local races.

Usually found settled on grass or weeds by the roadside, but it visits flowers, especially *Duranta*, and is very easy to catch.

214. TELICOTA AUGIAS. Also found in India, Burma, Malaya, Hong Kong, etc.

This has not been previously recorded from Ceylon, having been mistaken for *T. bambusæ*.

Elwes and Edwards say that it differs from *bambusæ* in having the "lower outer angle of the yellow spots in cells 2 to 4 narrowly produced along the contiguous vein nearly or quite to the termen ; terminal dark band brown." Whereas in *bambusæ* the "lower angle of the yellow spots in cells 2 to 4 is not, or but, little produced ; terminal margin black-brown."

The male can also be at once distinguished from male *bambusæ* by having narrow yellow streaks along all the veins at the apex of the fore wing. As pointed out by Elwes and Edwards, there is a marked difference in their clasps. See Plate 5, figs. 25 and 26.

The female is a much duller insect than female *bambusæ*, the ground colour being dark brown, not black-brown, and the orange markings being narrower. The spots in interspaces 1 to 3 have their lower edges produced along the contiguous veins, but to a much less extent than in the males. The veins at the apex of the fore wing are not edged with yellow. The under side of the hind wing has a marked greenish tinge.

In the great majority of Indian specimens that I have examined it differs both externally and internally from *bambusæ*, as in Ceylon specimens, but I have seen one male specimen that I could not place with certainty. The females are more difficult to sort, the greenish colour of the under side of the hind wing being the most constant distinction, in those that I have seen.

It is very common at times at Haldummulla. The larva feeds on sugar cane which is extensively cultivated in native gardens here. I have also specimens from Galle and Wellawaya.

215. TELIÇOTA (PADRAONA) GOLA, E. *Padraona goloides*, M. Found also in India, Malaya, China, Dutch Indies, etc.

Moore says *goloides* is "nearest allied to *P. gola*. Differs from it on both sides in the narrower discal band of the fore wing, the band being also disconnected from the costal spots. The band of the hind wing is also narrower." My series show considerable variation in the width of the band in both sexes, and it is connected to the pre-apical spots in a few of my males. The prehensores are similar to those of *P. gola*, as figured by Elwes and Edwards.

Mr. T. R. Bell points out that its early stages resemble those of an *Ampittia* more than a *Telicota*. The genitalia are very distinct from those of any Ceylon *Telicota*.

It is almost always found settled on grass by the roadsides, or at flowers, and is especially attracted by *Duranta*. If disturbed, it darts off very rapidly, but usually settles again near, and is easy to catch. It is very common at Haldummulla all the year round, except in August and September. I have also taken it at Haputale, Galle, Kandy, and Vavuniya.

216 TELICOTA (PADRAONA) DARA PSEUDOMÆSA.

216*a*. TELICOTA (PADRAONA) DARA SATRA
217 TELICOTA MÆSIOIDES.

Elwes and Edwards group these as *Telicota dara*, but the great difference in the genitalia of *pseudomæsa* and *mæsioides* prove that there are at least two distinct species in Ceylon and there may be a third, (my 216*a*) see Plate 5, figs. 27 to 32. I have examined well over 100 specimens of 216 and 217 and have found very slight internal variation. In addition I have dissected over 50 specimens from various parts of India and find that there are apparently a large number of local races which differ slightly externally, but can be easily separated by the different form of the genitalia. Most of those I have so far examined have the clasp roughly shaped like a crab's claw ; these may be only races of *dara*. One form from Coorg is very distinct and, if the genitalia are of the slightest use as a guide, it must be a distinct species. I have examined 7 or 8 males and found no variation. A specimen from Burma is very closely allied. I think this is the species described by Lt.-Col. Evans as *palnia* in the "Journal of the Bombay Natural History Society," Vol. XXIII., p. 309.

In all our Ceylon forms the sex mark is a deep black streak of specialized scales above the middle of vein 1 of the fore wing. Pending a revision of the genus I have retained Moore's names.

1st, *T. pseudomæsa*. This is a large form. The yellow band on the fore wing is broken, the spots in 4 and 5 being never joined to the apical group, but usually to the discal in the male. On the lower wing the band is divided along the veins by brown lines. There is, as a rule, a small well-defined spot in 6, and sometimes a larger faint and diffuse one in 7. It varies much in size. In the female the yellow markings are much reduced, and the band on the fore wing is more broken, the spots in 4 and 5 being almost invariably well separated from both the apical and discal series. On the lower wing there is usually a very minute spot in 6. For prehensores see Plate 5, figs. 27 and 28. The clasp is very like Elwes and Edwards' figure of that of *dara*, but the tegumen is quite distinct.

This is extremely plentiful at Haldummulla, but I have no specimens from any other locality. My notes give many localities for *dara*, but I cannot say for certain to which one of the group they refer. It usually settles on grass by the roadsides, but visits flowers in bright sunshine.

2nd, *T. satra*. This may be a distinct race, but the slight differences in the genitalia rather point to its being a seasonal form of *pseudomæsa*.

The ♂ closely resembles the ♀ *pseudomæsa* on its upper surface, and I had placed it as such in my collection till I noticed the sex mark. It resembles the figure of *P. satra* in "Lepidoptera Indica' fairly well. Fruhstorfer says *satra* is confined to Ceylon.

The yellow band is very narrow, and the spots in 4 and 5 are well separated from both the discal and apical series. There is a spot in 7, but none in 6. The band on the hind wing is not divided by brown lines. The female has the yellow markings greatly reduced, and the band on the hind wing is broken up by brown lines along the veins. The under side of the hind wing in both sexes has a very distinctive greenish tinge, which is, I believe, typical of *dara*. The prehensores differ slightly from those of *pseudomæsa*, but the differences appear to be constant; however, I have so far only been able to dissect six males. See Plate 5, figs. 31 and 32.

I have taken it at Haldummulla, in March and May.

3rd, *T. mæsioides*. This is a small form. The clasp is near that of *T. rectifasciata* but the sex mark of the male is quite distinct.

The yellow band is almost always continuous, the spots in 4 and 5 being joined to both the discal and apical series; it, however, varies greatly in width. The band on the hind wing is not divided by brown lines along the veins. There is almost invariably a large spot in 7, but very rarely one in 6. In the female the yellow markings are much reduced, and the spots in 4 and 5 are not always joined to the apical series. I have caught one aberration of the female, now in the British Museum collection, in which the spots in 4 and 5 are quite obsolete, and the discal band almost so. I took it at Anuradhapura in company with normal specimens.

It is not so plentiful as *pseudomæsa* at Haldummulla, but is very abundant in the Galle District. I have also taken it at Anuradhapura, Vavuniya and Mannar.

218. HALPE CEYLONICA.

218*a*. HALPE EGENA, E. *Halpe brunnea*, M.

Halpe egena is restricted to Ceylon. *H. ceylonica* is also found in Southern India.

According to Moore, who described *brunnea* (=*egena*) from a single female specimen, the chief distinction between it and *ceylonica* lies in the ground colour, which is " dark vinous brown " in *brunnea*, and " dark brown, base of wings and body olive-brown," in *ceylonica*.

Elwes and Edwards distinguish them by the discal band on the under side of the hind wing, which is brownish-yellow and very indistinct, in *egena*, and yellowish-white, and clearly defined, in *ceylonica*. The colour of the discal band is usually as they state, but it varies greatly in definition, and I have specimens of *ceylonica* in which it is so diffuse as to be almost indistinguishable. My experience is that the ground colour is the only reliable test. In the specimen of *egena* described by Moore the discal band was evidently exceptionally indistinct. As a rule, the spots on the fore wing are larger in *ceylonica*, but they vary much in size in both. In *ceylonica* ♂ the pre-apical spots vary from 1 to 3 in number, but the discal spots vary only in size. I have a specimen of *egena* ♂ with the wing entirely unspotted. The spot in the cell is rarely present in *egena* ♂, and rarely absent in *ceylonica* ♂. I can perceive no difference whatever in the prehensores. See Plate 5, figs. 33 and 34. In Indian forms of *Halpe*, local races are, in my experience, more easily distinguished by the prehensores than by external features.

The females are much rarer than the males, and the material at my disposal is rather limited. Apart from the ground colour, the chief difference between them seems to be the spots in interspace 1 of the fore wing. I have so far examined 25 *ceylonica* ♀ and 6 *egena* ♀. The usual marking in *ceylonica* is apparently one spot visible above and 2 below, but one or more of these are sometimes absent, and I have two specimens in which this interspace is quite unspotted. In 5 *egena* ♀♀ the interspace is unmarked, but in one specimen there is a white spot visible above and below. Personally I can find no reliable tests for separating the two forms, except by the ground colour when freshly caught, and I strongly suspect them to be only seasonal varieties of the same insect.

H. ceylonica I have never taken this myself, but the native collectors seem to be able to get the males in any quantity at Kandy; females are apparently scarce. It is also common at Ratnapura, and Mr. Hannyngton has sent me a specimen from Coorg, which seems to be identical, It is distinct, both externally and internally, from *H. moorei*, though closely allied

" Numerous at Kandy in the latter part of the year, and found at Pundaluoya." (F. M. Mackwood).

H. egena. This was originally described by Felder from " Kalupahana, Ceylon," and I think there can be little doubt that this estate was meant. The gentleman who was Superintendent then (Mr. R. E. Pineo) told me that naturalists used frequently to stop with him on their way to collect in the Bintenna country. I have taken it on the estate.

It is a very local fly, and was formerly always plentiful on a *Duranta* hedge at the bungalow on Blackwood estate, 2 miles from here. This hedge has now been cut out, but a few specimens may still be taken in the garden there, in July-August and November-December. I have also taken it on the Haldummulla-Horton Plains bridle road, and received specimens from Ratnapura.

It is attracted by Heliotrope blossom.

219. HALPE DECORATA.

Peculiar to Ceylon and confined to the wettest zone. I have never taken it myself, but have received a lot of males from Ratnapura. The female is extremely rare. It is described in "Lepidoptera Indica" See Plate 2, fig. 6.

On the upper side the fore wing differs from that of the male in having an orange spot above vein 1, and the orange patch in the cell is much reduced in size. On the lower wing the large median yellow patch is much reduced, or even sometimes entirely obsolete. All markings are much darker in colour. The ground colour of the under side is entirely different, being brownish-red instead of gamboge yellow; the spots on the fore wing agree with those on the upper side, except that that on vein 1 is more diffuse. On the lower wing the small black spots are usually very indistinct or absent but when present they correspond in position with those of the male. I figure the prehensores on Plate 5, figs. 35, and 36.

"Very abundant in Ratnapura, and parts of Ambegamuwa. Caught also at Labugama and Kottawa. Females very scarce" (F. M. Mackwood).

220. PARNARA (BAORIS) PENICILLATA, M. *Baoris oceia*, E.

This species is confined to Ceylon. Externally it mainly differs from the Indian *farri* in never having any spots in the cell of the fore wing. Internally the clasp differs constantly from that of all the specimens I have examined from India and Burma. See Plate 5, figures 37 to 40. It is a good species. Evans says (Journal of the "Bombay Natural History Society," Vol. XXIII., p. 309): "Dr. Chapman has dissected fourteen specimens, and finds that there are four species under the name *oceia*, viz., *oceia*, confined to the Philippines; *leechii*, El., confined to China; *farri*, M., the common Indian species; *unicolor*, M., from Sikkim and Assam, a species with no markings on the fore wing." He unfortunately did not examine a Ceylon specimen.

The few males in my collection vary in the number of spots on the fore wing; in one there are spots in 2, 3, 4, 6, 7, and 8, the latter being very minute; in another there are spots in 2 and 3 only. The cell of the fore wing and the whole hind wing are unspotted in all. All the specimens of *farri* from India and Burma which I have seen have 2 spots in the cell of the fore wing.

The female is very likely to be mistaken for the female of *P. cahira lanka,* but it differs in the ground colour, especially of the under side. This is distinctly greenish-brown of a darker tint than that of *P. seriata.* Expanse about 42 mm. Spots on the fore wing in 1, 2, 3, 4, 6, 7, and 8. Cell of the fore wing and under side of hind wing unmarked. On the under side of the fore wing there is only one small diffuse spot in interspace 1.

It is very rare and apparently confined to the wet zone, I have specimens from Galle, Deniyaya, Ratnapura, and Avisawella. Mr. Mackwood also gives Punduloya and Lindula as localities.

221. PARNARA (CHAPRA) MATHIAS AGNA. *Chapra agna*, M.

221*a*. PARNARA (CHAPRA) MATHIAS SUBOCHRACEA. *Chapra mathias*, M. *P. mathias*, or races thereof, is found all over Asia and in Australia. The type of *subochracea* is from Calcutta.

Moore gives *mathias* and *agna* from Ceylon, and says *agna* is larger than *mathias,* and has smaller spots. Personally I find that the form with the small spots is usually the smaller insect. Elwes and Edwards agree with Moore in dividing it into two species, naming the one with the small spots *mathias,* and the one with the large *subochracea.* There are certainly two distinct forms in Ceylon which are extremely common; they fly together, and the males, at any rate, do not seem to grade.

a. agna. Smaller and darker. ♂ spots in fore wing in 2, 3, 4, 6, and 7 and very rarely in 8. No spot in 5. Two spots in cell The spot in 2 at least twice as high as broad. ♀ spots larger than in ♂. Two in 1 and one in 2, 3, 4, 5, 6, 7 and 8. That in 5 is sometimes missing. Under side hind wing: Spot in cell and almost always four or more discal spots; that in 6 being no larger than the others.

b. subochracea. Larger, wings broader and paler. ♂ spots on fore wing in 2, 3, 4, 6, 7, and 8, and very rarely in 5. That in 8 is sometimes missing. Two spots in cell. The spot in 2 is roughly quadrate, at least as broad as high. ♀, wings much broader than in *agna.* Spots similar, but that in 6 on the under side of the hind wing usually more prominent than the others.

c. Much smaller than last but markings similar. Under side heavily suffused with grey. I believe it to be the dry season form of *subochracea.*

The differences in the prehensores of *a* and *b* are exceedingly minute and hard to see, though apparently constant. The chief one lies, as pointed out by Elwes and Edwards, in the apex of the tegumen.

I have examined a good series of allied forms from Kanara, they do not differ as much as ours, and the genitalia are even harder to differentiate. I have also had about a dozen ♂♂ from other parts of India, but they seemed identical with Kanara forms. I have seen no typical *subochracea,* so may have named form *b* wrongly The spot in 5 on the fore wing in the ♀♀ does not appear to be so common in Indian specimens as in ours.

Form *c* is very rarely found except in the North of the Island (dry zone) The other forms fly all the year round at Haldummulla and are always plentiful.

222. PARNARA (CALTORIS) CAHIRA LANKA, E. *Parnara kumara,* M. The type of *kumara* is from Kanara Our form may be classed as a local race, it differs sufficiently from specimens from Kanara, but those from Coorg seem to be intermediate. I append a description of our form. The chief distinction seems to be that the under side of the hind wing of the ♀ is always unspotted.

Male—Expanse 40-45 mm. No spot in cell of fore wing; hind wing unmarked. Spots on the fore wing in 2, 3, 4, 6, and 7, some or all of the three latter being sometimes obsolete. Under side: Costa and apex of fore wing and the whole hind wing dark orange-brown, deepening in old or worn specimens into vinous brown. As a rule, there are no spots in interspace 1 of the fore wing below, but very rarely a small very diffuse one is present. I have three specimens in which there is a minute spot showing above on vein 1, but in colour, shape of the wings and prehensores they are identical with this species.

I have dissected many specimens with both bright and dull coloured under sides and find the prehensores to be identical. See Plate 5, figs. 41 to 44. The clasp answers exactly to Elwes and Edwards' illustration of that of *austeni*, the tegumen, however, is quite distinct from that of either *austeni* or *kumara* though nearer to that of the former.

Female—Expanse 42-48 mm. Spots on fore wing in 1, 2, 3, 4, 6, 7, and 8. The spot in 8 is sometimes missing, and there is occasionally a second minute spot in 1 just below vein 2. The wings are broader in proportion to their length, the termen and dorsum of the fore wing being almost equal. The colour of the under side and cilia are identical with No. 224. There is always a diffuse spot in interspace 1 below, and often a second very minute one touching vein 2. The hind wing is always unspotted.

I have examined several specimens from Coorg and Kanara. The prehensores are extremely near to those of our form, the clasp seems to be identical, but the tegumen differs slightly. The males from Coorg are like ours, but the 4 males from Kanara all showed a minute spot above vein 1 of the fore wing. This is extremely rare in Ceylon specimens. Moore says, the female *kumara* has on the under side of the hind wing "an indistinct yellow discal spot between the two lower median veins." I have never found this spot in Ceylon specimens, but it is present in all the Coorg females that I have examined, and in one from Coorg, and in all those from Kanara, it is very distinct, and there is also a smaller spot in interspace 3.

I have one very battered specimen of a female from Haldummulla, which shows no spot in interspace 1 of the fore wing above, and only a small very diffuse one below.

It is a hill insect and occasionally appears in great numbers on the Haldummulla-Horton Plains bridle road, and a few can be taken as low as 3,000 feet here. It is abundant on the hills above Ratnapura. It usually settles low along the roadsides, and does not fly far if disturbed.

Through the courtesy of Mr. Joicey I have been able to examine the genitalia of *P. cahira* from the Andamans. From these it is quite clear that our form is a race of *cahira,* as pointed out by Lt.-Col. Evans.

222*a*. PARNARA (CALTORIS) CAHIRA AUSTENI.

This is given as a Ceylon species by Elwes and Edwards on the authority of Mr. E. E. Green. I fancy it has been confused with the preceding as the clasp of our *kumara* is identical with Elwes and Edwards' figure of that of *austeni.* Apparently *austeni* differs from *kumara* in always having one or two spots in the cell of the fore wing, and I have seen nothing answering to that description in Ceylon.

223. PARNARA (CALTORIS) PHILLIPPINA SERIATA. *Parnara seriata*, M.

The type of *phillippina* is from the Philippines, that of *seriata* from Ceylon. Moore describes it as " smaller than *kumara*, the spots smaller and less angular. Under side greenish-brown, not deep ochreous-brown."

Through the courtesy of Mr Joicey I have been able to examine six specimens of *phillippina* from the Philippines, and also Mr. Edwards' original dissections for Messrs. Elwes and Edwards' work. The differences between *phillippina* and *seriata*, both external and internal, are very small, and I consider that the latter is, at most, only a local race, if it can be separated at all. The spots on the fore wing seem to be smaller and less angular in *seriata.* The prehensores are figured on Plate 5, figs. 45 to 48.

Description of our form of *seriata.*

Male—Expanse 36 to 42 mm. Spots on fore wing above in 1, 2, 3, 4, 6 and 7. In two of my specimens there is also a minute dot in 1, just below vein 2 In a few others the spot on vein 1 is almost obsolete. No spot in cell. Underside: Spots on fore wing as above except that there are always *two* diffuse spots in 1. I have seen two specimens which showed a rudimentary spot in the cell which did not show above. Costa, apex of fore wing, and whole of hind wing brown, irrotated with yellow scales, giving a marked greenish tinge.

Female—Expanse 42-45 mm. Spots on fore wing in 1, 2, 3, 4, 6, 7, and 8 There is also a second very small spot in 1, just below vein 2. The spot in 8 is sometimes missing. No spots in cell visible above. Under side: Two large diffuse spots in 1. Many specimens also show rudimentary spots in the cell, of which the lower is the larger.

A variety may be taken which has a single white spot on the under side of the hind wing in interspace 2, sometimes visible above; the spot below vein 2 on the upper side of the fore wing is enlarged into a streak almost reaching the spot on vein 1. I have five specimens of this variety from Galle, and one from Haldummulla, and have seen others from Ratnapura. I have also a specimen from Galle which only shows the white spot on one wing.

I have examined a series from Kanara, which are almost identical both internally and externally. One female specimen shows the spot in interspace 2 of the hind wing.

It is found from sea level to about 3,000 feet elevation. I have specimens from Haldummulla, Galle, Kottawa, Ratnapura, Balangoda and Kandy. The native collectors can get the males in abundance at the latter place, but so far they have only sent me a single female.

224. PARNARA (CALTORIS) CONJUNCTA NAROOA, E. *Parnara narooa*, M.

The type of *conjuncta* is from the Philippines, that of *narooa* from Bombay. *P. conjuncta*, or races thereof, is found in India, Burma, Malaya, Hong Kong, etc.

I have so far failed to get any specimens of *conjuncta* from the Philippines but I have examined several specimens from Kanara, which should be nearly typical *narooa*, and Mr. Joicey has lent me specimens from Java, Borneo, Nias, and Perak, and Mr. Edwards' dissections for Elwes and Edwards' work. Externally the chief difference seems to be the much larger spots on the under side of the hind wing in *narooa*. The genitalia differ very slightly if at all, see Plate 6, figs. 49-52 and *narooa* is only separable as a race at most. The genitalia show a close relationship to those of the *mathias* group, and the ♀ of the Ceylon form agrees with the ♀♀ of our *agna* and *subochracea* in usually having a spot in 5 of the fore wing, which seems to be rare in Indian and Far Eastern specimens.

It is not rare at Haldummulla, but is difficult to catch in first class condition. I have also taken it at Haputale, Madampe, and Galle, and have specimens from Ratnapura.

225. PARNARA (CALTORIS) COLACA, E. *Parnara cingala*, M. Moore thought it distinct from *colaca*, but did not state how it differed. I can detect no difference externally or internally in the few specimens I have examined from S. India. The prehensores are figured on Plate 6, figs. 56-58.

It is a very constant form in Ceylon, the main variation being in the number of spots in the cell; these may be two, one, or none; all varieties seem to be equally common in both sexes. The number of the spots on the fore wing outside the cell never seems to vary, being always one each in 1, 2, 3, 4, 6, 7 and 8. On the hind wing below there are always three spots in 2, 3, and 5, and usually a smaller one in 4; of these, one or two are, as a rule, visible above. Some varieties are very like *mathias* ♀, but can be distinguished by the absence of the small spots just below vein 2 and in 5 of the fore wing above, and of that in the cell of the hind wing below.

It is the commonest skipper at Haldummulla, and flies all the year round. I have also taken it at Ohiya (6,000 feet) Nuwara Eliya, Jaffna, Mannar, Galle, etc. It is chiefly found in the grass by the roadsides, and visits flowers when the sun is shining.

226. PARNARA BADA. Found also in India, Malaya, Burma, China, and Japan. Evans gives *guttatus* as a distinct species from Chitral and Assam; it differs mainly in its lighter colour and larger spots, especially on the hind wing. I am not sure that *bada* should not rank as a race of *guttatus*.

This is the smallest *Parnara* in Ceylon. It can be distinguished from *cingala*, which is only slightly larger, by the absence of the spot in interspace 1. The spots vary greatly in size, shape, and number. On the fore wing there are normally spots in 2, 3, 4, 6, 7, and 8, but those in 4 and 8 are often absent. I have one specimen with a spot in 5, and two with a linear spot on the lower edge of the cell, near the base of vein 3 On the hind wing there is normally a row of four spots in interspaces 2 to 4, visible both above and below. I have two specimens in which the hind wing is quite unspotted above or below, and several with only one to three minute spots below. I have also two or three with five discal spots in interspaces 2 to 5, and one in the cell. The spot in 5 is never in line with the others.

The antennæ are relatively much shorter than is usual in the *Parnaras*, and Mr T. R. Bell, I.F.S., has discovered that the larva and pupa shew a closer resemblance to those of the genus *Padraona.* The prehensores are figured on Plate 6, figs. 53-55. They are very distinct from those of any other Ceylon *Parnara.*

It is not very common at Haldummulla, but becomes much more abundant at lower elevations, being widely distributed through the low-country. I have taken it at Wellawaya Hambantota, Galle, Vavuniya, Jaffna, Mannar, etc., and have specimens from Kandy.

Ismeneinæ

227. ISMENE ATAPHUS, E. *Ismene œdipodea,* M. Also found in India and Burma.

I œdipodea differs in having the " costa of the hind wing folded over on to the upper surface of the apex " (Elwes and Edwards). It is found in Java and Sumatra.

Very rare in Uva, but well distributed. I have taken it at Ohiya (6,000 feet), Haldummulla (3,500 feet), and Hambegama tank (400 feet). It is fond of settling in the beds of streams, on wet rocks, or sand I have specimens from Kandy.

For prehensores see Plate 6, figs. 59 and 60.

228. HASORA BADRA. Found also in India, Burma, Malaya, Dutch Indies, China, etc.

I have taken a pair in my garden, but have seen no others in the Province of Uva. I have specimens from Ratnapura,

Kottawa, Deniyaya, and Kandy. I understand it is not rare at Balangoda, and has been taken in Nuwara Eliya.

The prehensores are figured on Plate 6, figs. 65 and 66

229. HASORA (PARATA) CHROMUS, M., E.

230. HASORA (PARATA) BUTLERI, E. *Parata alexis*, M. *H. butleri* is found also in Southern India. Races of *chromus* are found in India, Burma, Dutch Indies, etc.

A revision of the genus will probably result in both forms being divided into several local races. The present nomenclature does not seem satisfactory.

Elwes and Edwards treat them as varieties of *H. chromus*. The external differences are very marked, they fly together and do not grade, and their prehensores are widely different.

The clasp of *chromus* is the same as Elwes and Edwards' figure of that of *inermis*. I have examined a large number from Ceylon, India and the Andamans, and find it very constant. The tegumen shows signs of four rudimentary horns, see Plate 6, figs. 63 and 64. The clasp of *butleri* is that figured by Elwes and Edwards as *chromus*, and the tegumen has four long horns See Plate 6, figs. 61 and 62. It is practically identical in specimens from Ceylon and Kanara. I have had a few allied, but distinct forms from North India, but have only seen true *butleri* from South India and Ceylon. My material from anywhere else than Kanara and Ceylon has however been far too limited.

The upper sides of the males of our Ceylon forms are similar, but the under sides are very distinct, the most prominent difference being that *butleri* has a broad, sharply defined, white band on the lower wing, and *chromus* has a narrow diffuse one. The female of *butleri* has, as a rule, two small white spots on the upper side of the fore wing in 2 and 3, of which the lower is much the smaller, but both these spots are often absent. In this case the ♂ can only be distinguished from the ♀ by the absence of the sex mark. This form of female is sometimes mistaken for the male of *H. chabrona*, which I do not believe to be found in Ceylon. The female of *chromus* has two spots in all my specimens, of which the lower is the larger. It has also occasionally a minute spot in interspace 6.

Mr. Hannyngton sent me a *chromus* ♀ from Coorg. It is larger than our Ceylon forms, the spots in 2 and 3 are much larger, and there is a spot in 6 and a small dot in 7. The band on the hind wing is broader than that of *alexis*, but is not sharply defined like that of *butleri*.

They suddenly appear in great numbers, generally during the north-east monsoon, and I am of opinion that they "flight." In October, 1916, I noticed great flights of large *Hesperiidæ* on several evenings just before dark, all going south. I put on two native collectors and tried myself to catch specimens, but owing to the bad light and the speed of the flight I secured none. They can be walked up in the daytime in the tea or jungle, but then only fly a short distance, and settle on the under side of a leaf with their wings closed over their backs. They visit flowers in the early morning or evening or on a dull day, and I have known them come to my moth lamp at night.

Both are extremely plentiful all over Uva, up to the highest elevations, and I have specimens of *butleri* from Kandy and Deniyaya, and of *chromus* from Kandy, Jaffna and Mannar.

231. BIBASIS SENA. Also found in India and Siam.

The colour of the cilia on the hind wing and the patch of long hairs on the dorsum, above the tornus, varies from rather pale orange to orange-vermilion in freshly caught specimens. The fore wing of the female is broader than that of the male, and the hind wing is more rounded.

I consider it a rarity. I have taken one or two specimens on this estate, and in December, 1904, I found several inside Wellawaya resthouse settled on the walls. They were very wary and difficult to catch, so I only got three or four; the others did not return to the resthouse that day. With these exceptions, I have never come across it, but have received specimens from Kandy.

The prehensores are figured on Plate 6, figs. 69 and 70.

232. BADAMIA EXCLAMATIONIS. Also found in India, Burma, Malaya, China, and Australia.

It appears in great numbers at times, usually in company with *H. alexis* and *butleri*. It has the same habits as these, but seems to be less afraid of the sun, and to visit flowers more on a bright day.

I have notes of its occurrence at Haldummulla, Haputale, Kandy, Galle, Vavuniya, and Mannar, and believe it to be common everywhere at times.

The prehensores are figured on Plate 6, figs. 71 and 72. That of the clasp is poor, as it does not show the formidable armament of spines on the inner face. I have noticed no variation in about a dozen specimens from various parts of India.

233. RHOPOLACAMPTA BENJAMINII, E. *Choaspes benjaminii.* M. Found also in India, Burma, China, Japan, Borneo, etc.

There seems to be a doubt as to whether two species are not included under this name, I therefore figure the prehensores of our Ceylon form, Plate 6, figs. 67 and 68. Those of the specimens from the Khasia Hills and Chatak that I have examined differ slightly.

It is fairly common in the hills, and was formerly very plentiful on the cart road below the Haputale jungle, but since the Forest Department has cleaned out the original vegetation and planted Eucalyptus in its place, this and other hill butterflies have, of course, disappeared. It is still common between Haputale and Ohiya, and I have specimens from Maskeliya, the hills above Ratnapura, and Kandy. I have taken it as low as 3,500 feet at Haldummulla.

When walking in the jungle near the Mocha Patanas, Maskeliya, with the late Mr. John Pole, he pointed out the larvæ to me feeding on a shrub, called by the Sinhalese there *hik*. I have been unable to identify this. The name *hik* is usually given to *Odina wodier*, a low-country tree.

The males are nearly always found settled on wet roads or in the beds of streams. They are strongly attracted by birds' droppings. The females are difficult to procure.

ADDENDA

The *atrata* group of the genus *Nacaduba.*

I have submitted specimens of the genitalia of the Ceylon members of this group to the British Museum (Nat. Hist.). Capt. Riley agrees with me that we have four distinct forms, and asked me to name the new one. I call it *Nacaduba sinhala.*

Adopting Fruhstorfer's names for the others, our list will now stand as follows :—

92. NACADUBA SINHALA. *Mihi.* This is my form "a"—See page 53.

93. NACADUBA PERUSIA PROMINENS. *Fruh.* My form "b."

94. NACADUBA BERENICE CEYLONICA. *Fruh.* My form "c."

94a. NACADUBA ATRATA GYTHION. *Fruh.* My form "d."

APPENDIX A.

List of butterflies the larvæ of which are believed to feed on cultivated plants. Where not specified the leaves are attacked.

A. Known to feed on paddy.

ORSOTRIOENA MANDATA

MYCALESIS PERSEUS TYPHLUS.

MYCALESIS MINEUS POLYDECTA.*

MELANITIS LEDA.

PRECIS ALMANA.*? *See note B.*

AMPITTIA MARO.

TELICOTA AUGIAS.*

PARNARA MATHIAS AGNA.

PARNARA MATHIAS SUBOCHRACEA.

PARNARA COLACA.

PARNARA BADA.

Note B. *P. almana* is recorded in India "on one occasion in large numbers destroying rice fields" but "this record requires confirmation." (Proceedings of 2nd Entomological Meeting, Pusa, p. 163.)

B. Larvæ feed on grasses, cultivated or wild, and will probably attack paddy at times.

MYCALESIS SUBDITA

NISSANGA PATNIA

LETHE DYRTA NILGIRIENSIS

YPTHIMA SINGALA

YPTHIMA CEYLONICA

MELANITIS PHEDIMA TAMBRA

BARACUS VITTATUS

IAMBRIX SALSALA

TARACTROCERA MÆVIUS

TELICOTA BAMBUSÆ.

TELICOTA GOLA.

TELICOTA MÆSIOIDES.

TELICOTA DARA PSEUDOMÆSA.

PARNARA CONJUNCTA NAROOA.

C. Cultivated plants other than paddy.

EUPLŒA CORE ASELA ..	Oleander.
ELYMNIAS HYPERMNESTRA FRATERNA ..	Palms. Often reported as a pest of ornamental pot palms.
ELYMNIAS SINGHALA ..	Palms.
CHARAXES FABIUS ..	Tamarind.
EULEPIS ATHAMAS AGRARIUS	Albizzia moluccana. Where grown as green manure.

C. Cultivated plants other than paddy.—*Contd.*

EUTHALIA VASANTA	..	Mango and cashew.
MODUZA CALIDASA	..	Cinchona.
NEPTIS VARMONA	..	Vigna catjang.*
PRECIS ORITHYIA	..	Sweet potato.
PRECIS LEMONIAS	..	" Found at Pusa on Sida rhombifolia and at Nagpur on jute."*
CETHOSIA NIETNERI	..	Passion flowers.
HYPOLIMNAS MISIPPUS	..	Portulaca oleracea.
VANESSA HARONICA	..	Wild yams, and will probably attack cultivated species.
ARGYNNIS HYPERBIUS TAPROBANA	..	Violets.*
ERGOLIS TAPROBANA	..	Castor oil plant.
ACRÆA VIOLÆ	..	Cucurbitaceæ. Occasionally a pest of cucumbers and gourds. Hibiscus cannabium.
ZIZERA OTIS ..	..	Gram and sesbania aculeata.
CHILADES LAIUS	..	The young shoots of orange, lime, etc.
CHILADES TROCHILUS F. PUTLI ..	..	Indigo and pea pods.*
LAMPIDES BOCHUS	..	The pods of various peas, beans and pulses. A pest of Boga medelloa when grown for green manure.
LAMPIDES ELPIS	..	" A decided pest of cardamoms."* They attack the flowers and young fruit and the great number often seen in cardamom clearings proves that the damage done must be very great.
LAMPIDES BOETICUS	..	Peas and beans. A pest of Crotalaria when grown as green manure. Attacks the pods.
CATACHRYSOPS STRABO PANDAVA	..	Cycads.
EUCHRYSOPS CNEJUS	..	The pods of gram, peas, beans, etc.
TARUCUS THEOPHRASTUS ..	..	Ziziphus jujuba. " A minor pest of grafted Ber trees."*
CHLIARIA NILGIRICA	..	May damage the blossoms of cultivated orchids.
CHERITRA FREJA JAFFRA ..	..	Cinnamon.
DEUDORIX EPIJARBAS	..	Very destructive to pomegranates. The larva lives inside the fruit.

C. Cultivated plants other than paddy.—*Contd.*

VIRACHOLA ISOCRATES ..	Luckily rare in Ceylon. In India known to spoil the fruits of pomegranate, wood-apple, orange, apple, loquat, guava, plums, peaches, tamarinds and nux vomica.*
VIRACHOLA PERSE ..	Said to attack the fruit of pomegranate.
RAPALA SCHISTACEA ..	Tea blossom.
CATOPSILIA CROCALE, POMONA, PYRANTHE, AND FLORELLA, AND TERIAS HECABE ..	Sometimes entirely defoliate various species of Cassia, Sesbania, etc.
TERIAS SILHETANA. ..	Albizzia moluccana.
PAPILIO DEMOLIUS ..	Orange and lime. In India "sometimes a serious pest, stripping the trees."*
PAPILIO MOOREANUS PAPILIO POLYMNESTOR PARINDA .. PAPILIO POLYTES ROMULUS ..	Orange and lime.
PAPILIO CLYTIA LANKESWARA ..	Cinnamon.
PAPILIO TEREDON ..	Cinnamon.
PAPILIO AGAMEMNON ..	Soursop and custard apple.
HESPERIA GALBA ..	"Sida rhombifolia, hollyhock, soy bean."*
SUASTUS GREMIUS ..	Palmyra, cocoanut and other palms.
GANGARA THYRSIS ..	Sometimes a minor pest of cocoanuts in India.
PADUKA LEBADEA ..	Palms.
UDASPES ALYSOS AND RESTRICTA	Wild gingers and may attack cultivated species.
UDASPES FOLUS ..	"Occasionally does a good deal of damage to ginger and turmeric" in India.*
TELICOTA BAMBUSÆ ..	Maize in Burma.*
TELICOTA AUGIAS ..	Sugar-cane.
PARNARA MATHIAS ..	Sann hemp. In Burma, maize and sugar-cane.*
HASORA CHROMUS ..	Castor oil plant.*
PARNARA PENICILLATA ..	Sugar-cane.

*Report of proceedings of 3rd Entomological Congress of Agricultural Research Institute at Pusa, Feb. 1920.

APPENDIX B.

Food plants of the larvæ of all Ceylon Butterflies, so far as known at present. Mainly taken from the writings of Moore, De Nicéville and Bell.

HESTIA JASONIA ..	"A climbing Ascelepidaceous plant allied to Hoya." (De N.)
DANAIDA EXPROMPTA ..	Unknown
" LIMNIACE ..	Asclepias, Calotropis, Hoya.
" SEPTENTRIONIS ..	Asclepiadaceæ
" CHRYSIPPUS ..	Asclepias, Calotropis
" PLEXIPPUS ..	Raphis, Ceropegea, Raphanus.
" AGLEA ..	Tylophora, Calotropis, Cryptolepis.
" FUMATA ..	Alleophania decipiens.
EUPLOEA CORE ASELA ..	Nerium, Ficus.
" CORUS ..	Unknown. Has often been bred but no record kept.
" KOLLARI SINHALA ..	Unknown. *Kollari* in India, is said to feed on Ficus.
" CORETA MONTANA ..	Unknown. *Coreta*, in India, is said to feed on Apocynaceæ.
ORSOTRIOENA MANDATA..	Grasses and Paddy
MYCALESIS PERSEUS TYPHLUS..	Do
" MINEUS POLYDECTA	Do
" SUBDITA ..	Do
" RAMA ..	A native catcher assures me that this feeds on bamboo.
NISSANGA PATNIA ..	Grasses and possibly paddy.
LETHE DYNSATE ..	Bamboo.
" DRYPETIS ..	Do
" NEELGHERIENSIS	Grasses and probably paddy.
" DARETIS ..	Bamboo.
YPTHIMA SINGALA ..	Grasses.
" CEYLONICA ..	Grasses? (never recorded as bred.)

Appendix

MELANITIS LEDA	..	Paddy and grasses.
„ PHEDIMA TAMBRA	..	Grasses and probably paddy.
ELYMNIAS HYPERMNESTRA FRATERNA	..	Palmaceæ.
„ SINGHALA	..	Do
DISCOPHORA LEPIDA	..	Bamboo.
CHARAXES PSAPHON	..	Unknown.
„ FABIUS	..	Tamarind tree *inter alia.*
EULEPIS ATHAMAS AGRARIUS	..	Albizzia moluccana. Cæsalpina.
APATURA PARISATIS CAMIBA	..	Celtis lycodoxylon (In India. Bell).
PARTHENOS CYANEUS	..	Modecca. Passion flowers.
EUTHALIA NAIS	..	Diospyros. Shorea robusta (sal.)
„ EVELINA	..	Unknown.
„ LUBENTINA	..	Loranthus.
„ VASANTA	..	Mango, Cashew.
MODUZA CALIDASA	..	Rubiaceæ, Cinchona, Mussænda.
NEPTIS JUMBAH	..	Byttneriaceæ, Rhamnaciæ, Malvaceæ, etc.
„ VARMONA	..	Leguminosæ, Malvaceæ, Tiliaceæ.
RAHINDA SINUATA	..	Acacia.
PRECIS IPHITA	..	Acanthaceæ.
„ ATLITES	..	Do
„ ORITHYA	..	Do
„ HIERTA	..	Do
„ LEMONIAS	..	Do
„ ALMANA	..	Do Gloxinia Obseckia.
CUPHA PLACIDA	..	Flacourtia.
CETHOSIA NIETNERI	..	Modecca, Passion flowers.
CYNTHIA ASELA	..	Do
CIRROCHROA THAIS LANKA	..	Hydrocarpus.
HYPOLIMNAS BOLINA	..	Fleurya interrupta, Elatastemma cuneatum (Ind.)
„ MISIPPUS	..	Portulacca. Abutillon.
PYRAMEIS CARDUI	..	Urticaceæ, Compositæ, Malvaceæ, etc.
„ INDICA NUBICOLA	..	Heterophylla palmata, Urticaceæ.
VANESSA HARONICA	..	Smilax.

KALLIMA HORSFIELDI PHILLARCHUS ..	Acanthaceæ.
DOLESCHALLIA BISALTIDE	Do
ARGYNNIS HYPERBIUS TAPROBANA ..	Wild Violet.
ATELLA PHALANTA ..	Flacourtia, Smilax, Salix.
„ CEYLONICA ..	Alsodeia zeylanica, Violaceæ.
ERGOLIS MERIONE TAPROBANA ..	Tragia involucrata, Castor oil plant.
„ ARIADNE MINORATA ..	Tragia.
BYBLIA ILITHYIA ..	Tragia cannabina.
TELCHINIA VIOLÆ ..	Cucurbitaceæ. Modecca.
LIBYTHEA MYRRHA RAMA ..	Celtis.
„ LEPITA LEPITOIDES	Unknown.
ABISARA ECHERIUS PRUNOSA ..	Ardisia. Embelia (India).
———	
NEOPITHECOPS ZALMORA	Glycosmis (in India).
SPALGIS EPIUS ..	Carnivorous, Coccidæ.
MEGISBA MALAYA THWAITESI ..	Sapindaceæ.
CHILADES LAIUS ..	Rutaceæ.
„ PUTLI ..	Heliotropum strigosum. Lotus corniculatus.
LYCAENOPSIS AKASA ..	Unknown.
„ PUSPA ..	Xylia and Cylista (in S. India).
„ SINGALENSIS ..	Unknown.
„ LANKA ..	Smithia blanda.
„ LIMBATA ..	Unknown.
ZIZERA LYSIMON ..	Amaranthus. Zornia diphylla (India).
„ OTIS INDICA ..	Alysicarpus vaginalis. Zornia diphylla (India).
„ GAIKA ..	Nelsonia campestris and Lantana (S. India).
AZANUS UBALDUS ..	Acacia arabica and leucophlœa
„ JESOUS ..	Acacia leucophlœa.
LYCÆNESTHES LYCÆNINA ..	Wagatea spicata. Buchanania latifolia (in India).
TALICADA NYSEUS ..	Bryophyllum.
EVERES PARRHASIUS ..	Lotus corniculatus.

NACADUBA PACTOLUS CEYLONICA ..	Unknown.
,, PAVANA NABO	Do
,, VIOLA ..	Do
,, DANA ..	Do
,, PERUSIA PROMINENS ..	Vateria ?
,, ATRATA GYTHION ..	Wagatea spicata ?
,, BERENICE CEYLONICA..	Embelia ?
,, NORA ,, ,, ARDATES (TAILLESS)	Blossoms of Leguminosæ Sapındaceæ, Combretaceæ Myrtaceæ, etc.
,, NOREIA ..	Unknown.
JAMIDES BOCHUS ..	Boga medelloa, Xylea, Butea, etc.
LAMPIDES ELPIS ..	Flowers and young seeds of cardamoms, Kaempferia, etc.
,, CORUSCANS ..	Unknown.
,, LACTEATA ..	Do
,, CELENO ..	Leguminosæ, Abrus precatorius.
,, BOETICUS ..	Pods of Leguminosæ.
CATACHRYSOPS STRABO ..	Cylista scariosa, Dolichos, Ougeinia, etc.
EUCHRYSOPS CNEJUS ..	Pods of Leguminosæ.
CATACHRYSOPS PANDAVA LANKA..	Cycads.
,, CONTRACTA NILA ..	Unknown.
TARUCUS THEOPHRASTUS	Zizyphus.
SYNTARUCUS PLINIUS ..	Sesbania, Indigofera, etc.
CASTALIUS ROSIMON ..	Zizyphus rugosa.
,, ETHION ..	Zizyphus oenoplia (India).
,, DECIDEA ..	Do rugosa.
HORSFIELDIA ANITA NARADOIDES ..	Olax wightiana.
IRAOTA TIMOLEON ..	Ficus.
SURENDRA QUERCETORUM F. DISCALIS ..	Acacia pennata (India).
AMBLYPODIA CENTAURUS PIRAMA ..	Combretaceæ, Lythraceæ,
,, AMANTES ..	Leguminosæ, etc., where there are red ants' nests.
,, ORMISTONI	Unknown.
,, ABSEUS MACKWOODI	Do

CURETIS PHÆDRUS ..	Derris scandens, Xylia dolaori formis, etc.
ZESIUS CHRYSOMALLUS ..	Leguminosæ, Combretaceæ, etc., where there are red ants' nests.
CAMENA DEVA ..	Loranthus currula.
SPINDASIS LOHITA ..	Convolvulaceæ, Dioscoreæ, Terminalia.
,, VULCANUS FUSCA ..	Rutaceæ, Sapindaceæ, etc.
SPINDASIS SCHISTACEA ..	No record.
,, ICTIS ..	Do
,, NUBILUS ..	Do
,, LUNULIFERA ,, FAIRLIEI ..	Do
TAJURIA LONGINUS ..	Loranthus longiflorus.
,, JEHANA CEYLONICA ..	Unknown.
CHLIARIA NILGIRICA ..	Do , probably orchid blossoms.
CHERITRA FREJA JAFFRA	Cinnamon, Xylia, Leguminosæ.
RATHINDA AMOR ..	Ixora, and many others.
HORAGA ONYX CINGALENSIS ..	Onyx (in India) feeds on coriaria nepalensis.
CATAPOECILMA ELEGANS	Terminalia paniculata.
LOXURA ATYMNUS f. ARCUATA ..	Smilax, Dioscorea, etc.
DEUDORIX EPIJARBAS ..	Pomegranate and other fruits.
RAPALA SCHISTACEA ..	Euphorbiaceæ, Rosaceæ,
,, LAZULINA ..	Rhamnaceæ, Leguminosæ, etc., etc.
,, MELAMPUS ..	Ougeinia dalbergioides (in India).
,, LANKANA ..	Unknown.
BINDAHARA SUGRIVA .. ,,	Fruit of Salacea reticulata (Sing. himbatu). In India S. macrosperma.
VIRACHOLA ISOCRATES ..	Fruit of woodapple. A pest of many fruits in India.
,, PERSE ..	Fruits of Randia dumetorum, and others.

LEPTOSIA XIPHIA ..	Capparidæ.
DELIAS EUCHARIS ..	Loranthus.
PRIONERIS SITA ..	Capparidæ.
CATOPSILIA CROCALE ..	Leguminosæ, especially Cassia.
,, POMONA ..	Do do
,, PYRANTHE ..	Do do
,, FLORELLA ..	Do do

TERIAS LIBYTHEA ..	Leguminosæ
„ VENATA CINGALA	Do
„ HECABE ..	Do and others.
„ SILHETANA ..	Do , especially Albizzia.
„ ROTUNDALIS ..	Unknown.
IXIAS PYRENE CINGALENSIS ..	Capparidæ.
„ MARIANNE ..	Do
COLOTIS AMATA ..	Salvadoraceæ.
„ FAUSTA TRIPUNCTA ..	Capparidæ especially Maerua arenaria (India).
„ ETRIDA LIMBATA	Capparidæ
„ EUCHARIS ..	Do especially Cadaba indica.
„ DANÆ ..	Do do
ANAPHÆIS MESENTINA TAPROBANA ..	Do
APPIAS INDRA NARENDRA	Unknown, probably Capparidæ
„ ALBINA VENUSTA	Do do
„ PAULINA ..	Do do
„ LIBYTHEA ..	Capparidæ.
„ HIPPO TAPROBANA ..	Do especially Cratæva.
HEBOMOIA GLAUCIPPE AUSTRALIS ..	Capparidæ.
HUPHINA NERISSA EVAGETE ..	Do
„ NADINA REMBA	Do
PARERONIA VALERIA CEYLONICA	Do
TROIDES DARSIUS ..	Aristolochiæ.
PAPILIO HECTOR ..	Do
„ ARISTOLOCHIÆ CEYLONICA ..	Do
„ JOPHON ..	Do
„ DEMOLIUS ..	Rutaceæ, especially Citrus.
„ MOOREANUS ..	Do do
„ POLYMNESTOR PARINDA ..	Do do
„ POLYTES ROMULUS ..	Do do
„ CLYTIA LANKESWARA ..	Cinnamon, Laurineæ, Tetranthera.
„ CRINO ..	Satinwood tree, Meliaceæ.
„ ANTIPHATES ALCIBIADES ..	Unona lawii, Anonaceæ.

PAPILIO NOMIUS ..	Saccopetalum tomentosum, anonaceæ.
,, DOSON ..	Anonaceæ.
,, SARPEDON TEREDON ..	Laurineæ, Cinnamon.
,, AGAMEMNON MENIDES ..	Anonaceæ, custard apple, Magnolia.
HANTANA INFERNUS ..	Unknown.
SARANGESA ALBICILIA ..	Do
COLADENIA INDRANI TISSA ..	Xylia dolabriformis, Grewia microcos.
TAGIADES DISTANS ..	Unknown. Probably Dioscorea.
,, LITIGIOSA ..	Dioscorea. Smilax.
TAPENA THWAITESI ..	Doris and Dalbergia (in India).
CAPRONA RANSONNETTII	Helicteres isora (in India).
,, SIAMICA ..	Unknown.
GOMALIA ALBOFASCIATA	Do
HESPERIA GALBA ..	Sida rhombifolia, Waltheria indica.
BARACUS VITTATUS ..	Probably grasses.
SUASTUS GREMIUS ..	Palms.
,, MINUTA ..	Unknown.
IAMBRIX SALSALA ..	Grasses.
TARACTROCERA MÆVIUS	Unknown.
AMPITTIA MARO ..	Paddy and grasses.
HYAROTIS ADRASTUS ..	Rattan (in Sumatra).
MATAPA ARIA ..	Bamboo.
GANGARA THYRSIS ..	Palms.
PADUKA LEBADEA ..	Do
UDASPES FOLUS ..	Zinziberaceæ.
,, ALYSOS ..	Do
,, RESTRICTA ..	Do
TELICOTA BAMBUSÆ ..	Bamboo, grasses and paddy
,, AUGIAS ..	Sugar-cane.
,, GOLA ..	Grasses.
,, DARA PSEUDOMÆSA ..	Do
,, DARA SATRA ..	Probably grasses.
,, MÆSIOIDES ..	Grasses.
HALPE EGENA (=CEYLONICA) ..	Probably bamboo.
,, DECORATA ..	Unknown.

PARNARA PENICILLATA ..	Bamboo, sugar-cane.
,, MATHIAS AGNA	Paddy and grasses.
,, MATHIAS SUB-OCHRACEA ..	Paddy and grasses.
,, CAHIRA LANKA ,, PHILLIPPINA SERIATA. ..	These two species have been confused by various writers; apparently one feeds on grasses and paddy, and the other on bamboo.
,, CONJUNCTA NAROOA ..	Paddy and grasses.
,, BADA ..	Grasses and probably paddy.
,, COLACA ..	Do do
ISMENE ATAPHUS ..	Hiptage.
HASORA BADRA ..	Unknown.
,, ALEXIS ..	Pongamia, Heynia.
,, BUTLERI ..	Derris or Rourea (in India).
BIBASIS SENA ..	Combretum, Hiptage.
BADAMIA EXCLAMATIONIS ..	Terminalia, Ficus, Linociera, Combretum.
RHOPALOCAMPTA BENJAMINI.	Sabia and Meliosma (in India)

Index of Species

Index

Index

ERRATA

p. 53 line 28 lightly transparent
should be slightly transparent

p. 61 CATACHRYSOPS PANDAWA LANKA
should be CATACHRYSOPS PANDAVA LANKA

p. 97 APPIAS APULINA
should be APPIAS PAULINA

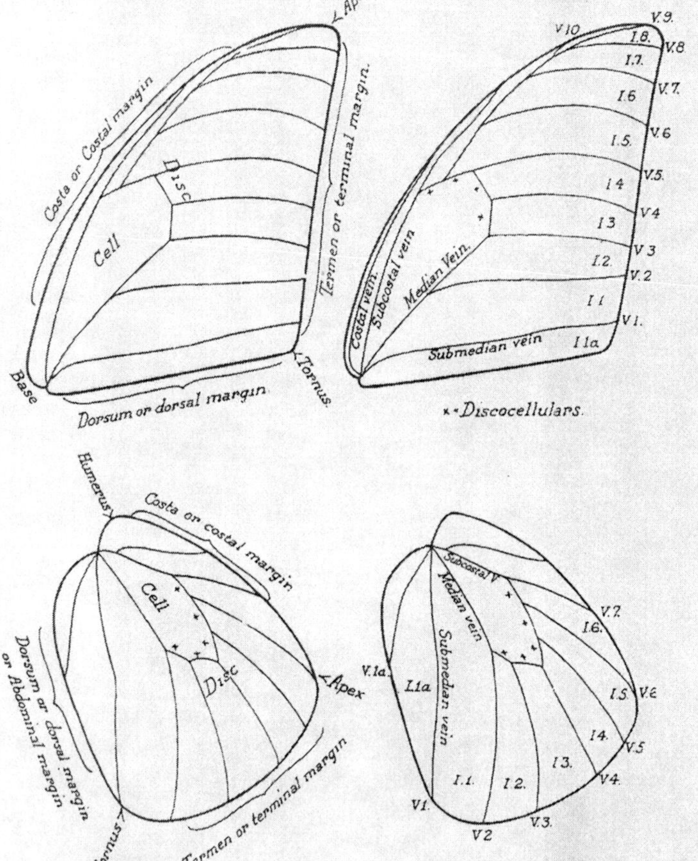

x = Discocellulars

V.1 V.2 &c Veins

I.1 I.2 &c Interspaces.

Adlard & Son & West Newman, Ltd., London.

Adlard & Son & West Newman, Ltd., London.

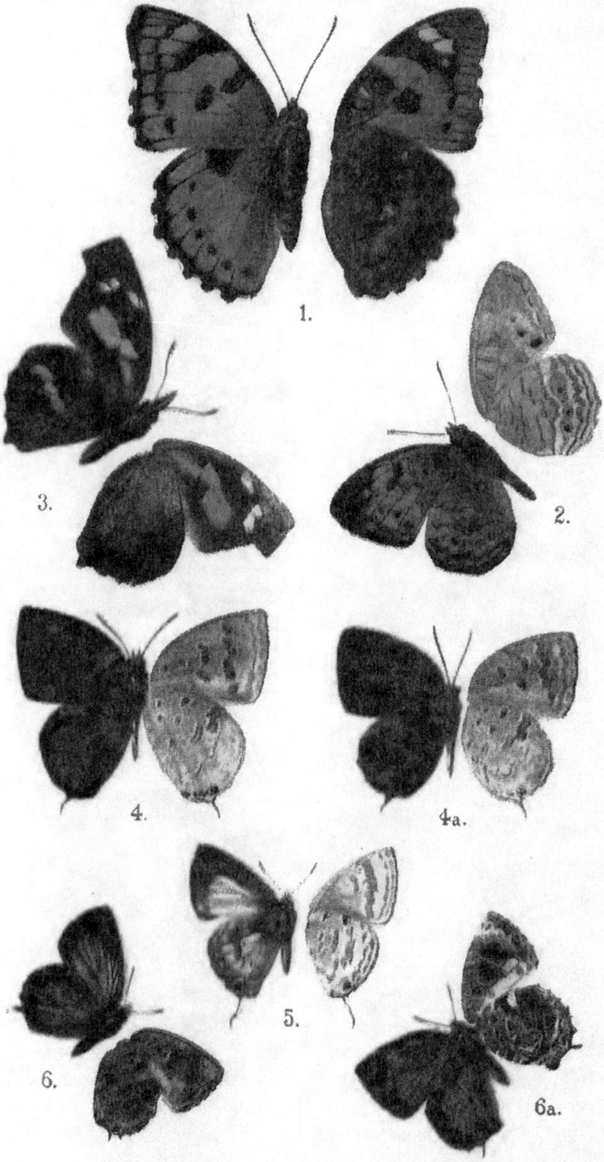

Adlard & Son & West Newman, Ltd., London.

PLATE III.

1. Terias libythea, warm season form
2. ,, ,, cold season form
3. Terias venata var. cingala ♂
4. ,, ,, ,, ,, ♀
5. ,, ,, var. rama ♂
6. ,, ,, ,, ,, ♀
7. Terias rotundalis ♂
8. ,, ,, ♀

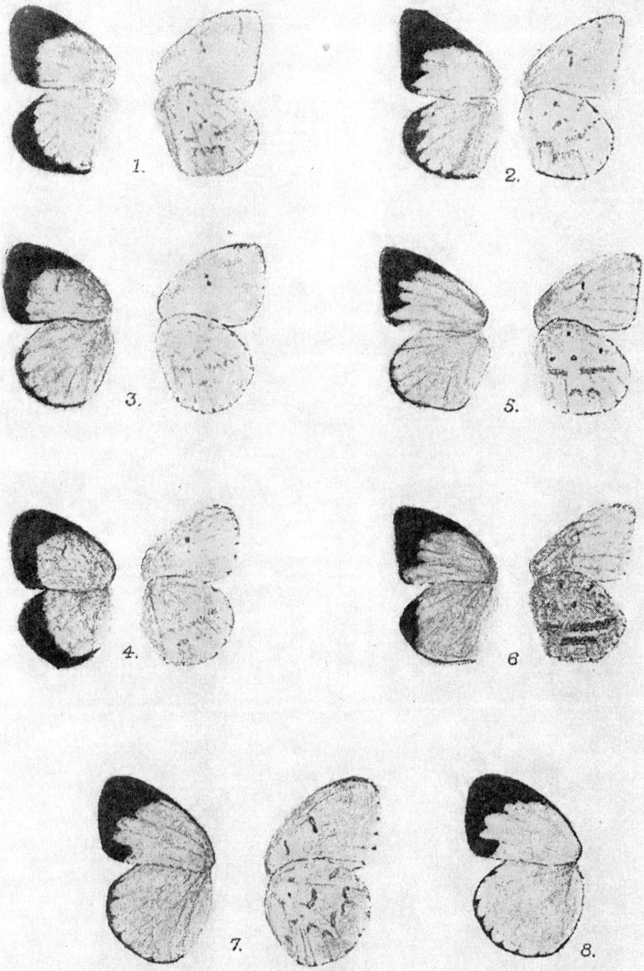

Adlard & Son & West Newman, Ltd., London.

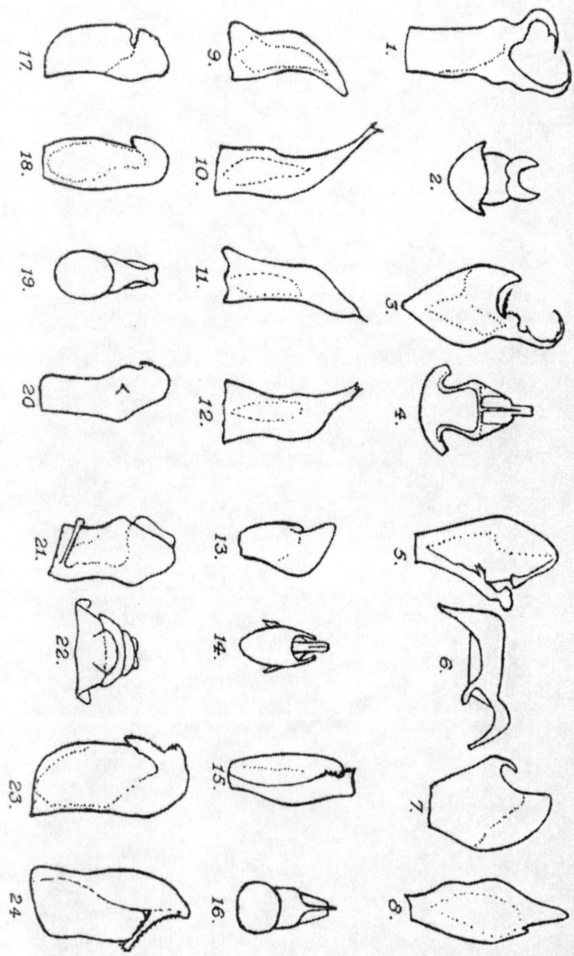

Adlard & Son & West Newman, Ltd., London.

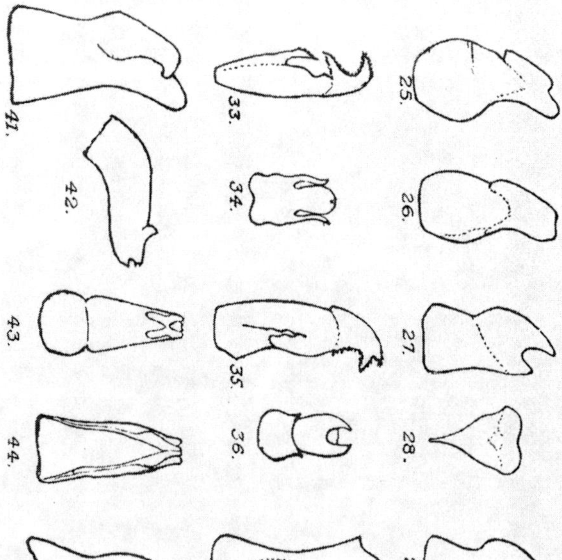

Adlard & Son & West Newman, Ltd., London.

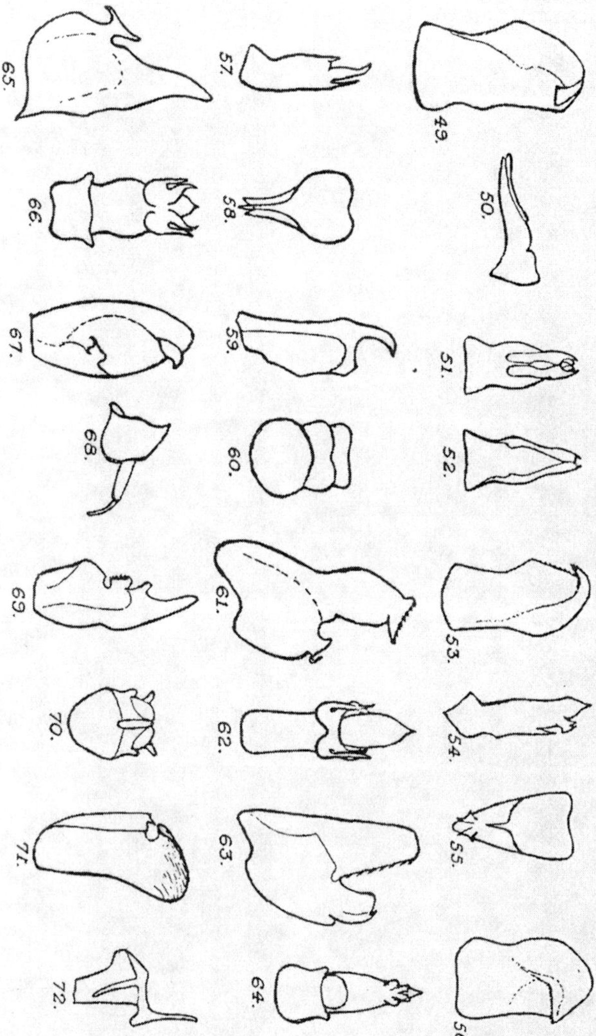

Adlard & Son & West Newman, Ltd., London.

PLATE VII.

Genitalia of some Ceylon Nacadubas.

---

1. Nacaduba pactolus ceylonica.
2. ,, pavana nabo, dry season form.
3. ,, ,, ,, wet season form.
4. ,, atrata gythion.
5. ,, perusia prominens.
6. ,, berenice ceylonica. lateral view.
7. ,, ,, ,, ventral view.
8. ,, sinhala.

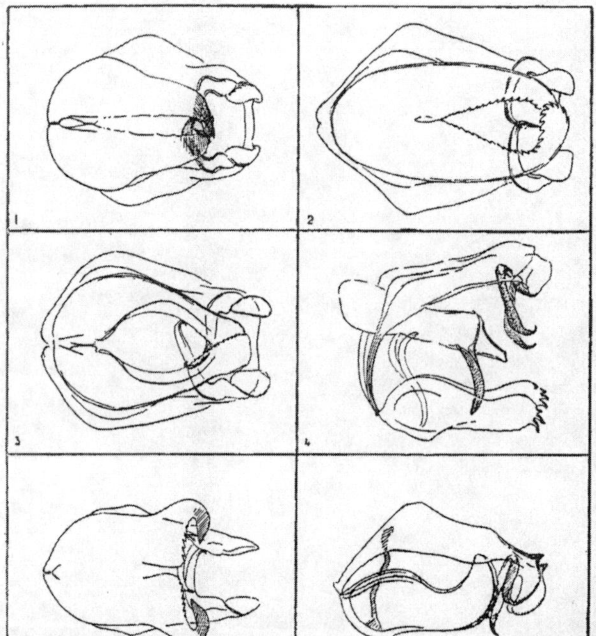
1
2
3
4
5
6
7
8